THE DINGLE PEN

A WALKING GUIDE

ADRIAN HENDROFF is a member of the Outdoor Writers and Photographers Guild, Mountain Training Association and Mountaineering Ireland. His articles and photographs have featured in *The Irish Times*, *Irish Examiner* and magazines such as *Trail, Outsider, Mountain World Ireland, Walking World Ireland, TGO, Irish Mountain Log, Trek & Mountain* and *Walking Wales Magazine*. For more information, visit Adrian's website and online gallery at www.adrianhendroff.com

You can also keep up to date at:

- facebook.com/adrianhendroff.exploreirelandsmountains
- twitter.com/exp_ireland_mtn

Also by Adrian Hendroff

From High Places: A Journey Through Ireland's Great Mountains
The Beara and Sheep's Head Peninsulas: A Walking Guide
The Dingle, Iveragh & Beara Peninsulas: A Walking Guide
Donegal, Sligo & Leitrim: Mountain & Coastal Hillwalks
Killarney to Valentia Island, The Iveragh Peninsula: A Walking Guide

Looking towards Sybil Point and The Three Sisters from the slopes of Cruach Mhárthain.

Disclaimer

Hillwalking and mountaineering are risk sports. The author and The Collins Press accept no responsibility for any injury, loss or inconvenience sustained by anyone using this guidebook.

Advice to Readers

Every effort is made by our authors to ensure the accuracy of our guidebooks. However, changes can occur after a book has been printed, including changes to rights of way. If you notice discrepancies between this guidebook and the facts on the ground, please let us know, either by email to enquiries@collinspress.ie or by post to The Collins Press, West Link Park, Doughcloyne, Wilton, Cork, T12 N5EF, Ireland.

Acknowledgements

There are several people whose encouragement, participation and support were invaluable during the making of this guidebook, and to whom I owe a huge debt of gratitude.

In particular, I would like to thank Tanya and Una, for the proof-reading and support. Thanks also to The Collins Press for your patience and continued support in my work, and for your expertise as always.

For your kindness, welcome and hospitality I should thank: Dave and Maria, Michael and Barbara, Denise Kane, Mick Sheeran, John Harte and Tim.

I'd like to acknowledge the following people for a number of reasons: Tony and Dianne from Australia, Christof and Katharina from Germany, John of 'Kool Scoops of Dingle', Pronsias of Midleton, Tom from Athlone, Dave Williams, John Fitzgerald and Stephen Bender.

For my friends, thank you for your friendship: Alan and Margaret Tees, Alun Richardson, Barry Speight, Charles O'Byrne, Colin Soosay, Conor O'Hagan, Conor Murphy, Gerry McVeigh, Iain Miller, John Noble, Martin McCormack, Maurice Harkin, Niamh Gaffney, Oisin Reid, Pat Falvey, Paul & Bairbre Duffy, Ray Chambers, Raymond and Suzanne Cummins, Richie Casey, Ronan Colgan, Steve Brown, Teena Gates and Tim McSweeney. Also in remembrance of my late friends Ian McKeever and Joss Lynam, and my grandfather RIP.

Finally to Kay and Una, a huge thanks for your love, patience and continuous support.

For those I may have forgotten to mention, please accept my apology in advance, as this is merely an oversight.

Edition notes

Due to ongoing access issues in Glanteenassig, the original Routes 20 and 21 have been replaced with new routes. A minor reroute is included for the start of Ballyduff to Anascaul (Route 14) and the start/finish of Beenbo *et al.* (Route 15) also due to access.

Beach at Ballyferriter and Ballydavid Head and the Brandon range to the right.

THE DINGLE PENINSULA
A WALKING GUIDE

ADRIAN HENDROFF

The Collins Press

For Niamh, Ciara and Joe

First published in 2015 by
The Collins Press
West Link Park
Doughcloyne
Wilton
Cork
T12 N5EF
Ireland

Reprinted 2016

Paperback ISBN: 978-1-84889-233-0

Design and typesetting by Fairways Design

Typeset in Myriad Pro

Printed in Poland by Białostockie Zakłady Graficzne SA

Contents

Route Location Map

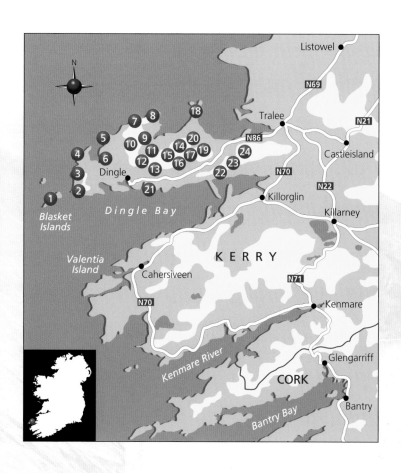

Listowel

N69

Tralee

N21

N86

Castleisland

N70

N22

Killorglin

Killarney

18

8

7

5

9

20

10

14

4

11

15

19

24

6

12

17

23

3

13

16

22

2

Dingle

21

1

Blasket
Islands

Dingle Bay

Valentia
Island

Cahersiveen

K E R R Y

N71

N70

Kenmare

Kenmare River

Glengarriff

CORK

Bantry

Bantry Bay

Quick-Reference Route Table

No.	Walk Name	Category
1	Great Blasket Island	
	Normal Route	Coastal Path and Hillwalk
	An Ceann Dubh Extension	Coastal Path and Hillwalk
2	Mount Eagle and Dunmore Head	Hillwalk
3	Cruach Mhárthain and Clogher Head	Mountain and Coastal Path, Hillwalk
4	Sybil Head and The Three Sisters	Coastal Hillwalk
5	Ballydavid Head and Beenmore	Coastal Hillwalk
6	Reenconnell	Mountain Path and Hillwalk
7	Piaras Mór and Masatiompan	Hillwalk
8	Sauce Creek from Brandon Point	Coastal Path and Hillwalk
9	Brandon Mountain from the East	Hillwalk
10	Brandon Mountain from the West	
	Normal Route	Hillwalk
	Longer Variation	Hillwalk
11	Brandon Mountain via Paternoster Lakes	Hillwalk
12	Ballysitteragh, Beennabrack and An Bhinn Dubh	Hillwalk
13	Slievanea loop from Conor Pass	Hillwalk
14	Ballyduff to Anascaul	Mountain Path and Hillwalk
15	Beenbo, Slievenagower, Slievenalecka and An Cnapán Mór	Hillwalk
16	Cnoc Mhaolionáin and An Bhánog Thuaidh	Hillwalk
17	Stradbally Mountain, Beenoskee, An Com Bán and Binn an Tuair	Hillwalk
18	Magharees Loop	
	Normal Route	Coastal Path
	Short Variation	Coastal Path
19	Glanteenassig Forest and Lakes	Forest Path
20	Stradbally to Beenoskee from Fermoyle Strand	Hillwalk
21	Bull's Head Loop from Kinard	Coastal Hillwalk
22	Knockbrack–Beenduff Ridge	Hillwalk
23	Derrymore Horseshoe	Hillwalk
24	Curraheen Horseshoe	Hillwalk

Grade	Distance	Ascent	Time	Page
3	9km	430m	3–3¾ hours	18
3	13.5km	670m	4½–5¾ hours	21
3	14.5km	600m	5–6 hours	23
2	12.5km	450m	4–5 hours	27
3	15.5km	450m	5–6 hours	31
3	8km	400m	2¾–3¼ hours	36
1	3.5km	205m	1–1½ hours	40
3	10km	800m	3¾–4¾ hours	43
3	13.5km	430m	4¼–5¼ hours	46
4	10km	980m	4–5 hours	50
3	7km	780m	3–3¾ hours	54
4	19km	950m	6½–8 hours	56
5	16km	1,080m	6½–7½ hours	57
3	11km	610m	3¾–4¾ hours	61
3	9.5km	540m	3¼–4 hours	64
2	13.5km	300m	4–5 hours	68
4	22km	900m	7–8¾ hours	72
3	10km	650m	3½–4½ hours	76
4	15km	910m	5¼–6½ hours	80
1/2	20.5km	N/A	5½–6½ hours	83
1	13.5km	N/A	3½–4½ hours	85
1	10.5km	150m	3–3¾ hours	87
4	25km	870m	8–10 hours	91
3	7km	400m	3–4hours	95
3	11.5km	510m	3¾–4¾ hours	99
4	11km	930m	4¼–5¼ hours	103
4	14.5km	880m	5½–6½ hours	108

Rocky coastline toward The Three Sisters (Route 4).

Introduction

My heart is looped around the rutted hills,
That shoulder the stars out of the sky,
And about the wasp-yellow fields,
And the strands where kelp-streamers lie;
Where, soft as lovers' Gaelic, the rain falls,
Sweeping into silver the lacy mountain walls.

                    – 'I am Kerry' by Sigerson Clifford (1913–1985)

From the sky, the Dingle Peninsula points to the sea like an outstretched finger. At the very edge of Europe, it extends from Tralee to Dunquin at its western tip for around 55km (34 miles), and is around 21km (13 miles) wide at its broadest. Voted among the Top 100 destinations in the world by TripAdvisor and referred to as 'the most beautiful place on earth' by *National Geographic*, its landscape is composed of soaring mountaintops, scenic hillside, secluded lakes, sweeping valleys, ancient ruins, dramatic sea cliffs, charming sea coves and long, sandy beaches.

Thirteenth-century records show the names of Dingle and *Daingean Uí Chúis* used in tandem. There are two interpretations of the meaning of its Irish equivalent. The Annals of the Four Masters refer to a chieftain named O'Cuis who ruled the area before the 1169 Norman invasion. However, it can be also taken to mean 'fortress of the Husseys', named after the arrival of a ruling Flemish family shortly after the invasion.

However, there is another name, one that cartwheels back in time: carved across the edge of several standing stones on the peninsula in Ogham, a fourth-century alphabet system named after Ogma, the Celtic god of eloquence, is found the name *Duibhne*, one of the Celtic goddesses associated with fertility and protection. Names are traditionally used as markers to define land boundaries, so the peninsula was then known as *Corca Dhuibhne*, or 'Duibhne's tribe'.

The landscape and bedrock of Dingle is much older than *Corca Dhuibhne*. Around 420 to 490 million years ago, during the Silurian and Ordovician Period, Ireland was under the Iapetus Ocean between two continents south of the equator. As plate tectonics pushed the continents closer, a collection of volcanic islands erupted, the lava and ash deposits of which can now be found at Clogher Head in the west of Dingle. Mud and sand sediments were deposited all over the peninsula, for example at Dunquin, Anascaul and near Camp.

The Iapetus had disappeared by the time of the Devonian, around 360 to 420 million years ago, and a large desert continent was formed. Younger, sandy sediments formed the Old Red Sandstone found today along the Slieve Mish Mountains. Older, coarser sediments resulted in conglomerates, evident at Inch and Glanteenassig.

The arid sandstone desert and conglomerates were then flooded by a shallow tropical sea during the Carboniferous Period, around 300 to 360 million years ago. The corals and shellfish that thrived then are now preserved in the limestone around the Magharees.

Finally, during the last ice age, only 10,000 years to 2 million years ago, sheets of ice advanced south from the Pole and covered most of northern Europe. The Dingle Peninsula was covered in thick ice sheets and glaciers. As the ice retreated, it scoured and sculpted the landscape, resulting in the deep U-shaped valleys, lake-filled corries and striated cliffs seen today in the Brandon, Conor Pass, Anascaul and Glanteenassig mountain areas.

It is this complex and intricate landscape, formed all those millions of years ago, which today gives the Dingle Peninsula its character and beauty. Defined by the combined magnetism of the mountains and the sea, the peninsula today attracts thousands of visitors annually, many of them walkers and outdoor enthusiasts. It is also an area rich with heritage, history and folklore: from Crom Dubh to Saint Brendan, from faery music to traditional Irish music, from holy wells to signal towers, and from Tom Crean to Tom Cruise.

The best way to get to know the Dingle Peninsula is to walk its byroads, walking trails, beaches, woodlands, valleys, coastline, clifftops, islands, hillside and mountains. This book attempts to do just that in a selection of 24 walking routes. These range from easy to difficult routes of various grades, and last from a few hours to full-day walks. The routes are designed to cover the length of the peninsula in a general west-to-east direction. Route selection has been tailored to be different from previous or existing guidebooks and a range of variations and extensions are also given. All routes have been checked in 2013 and 2014, with access foremost in mind. However, as access may be withdrawn at any time, if you do encounter any problems with any of the routes described in this book, please contact the publisher and myself so we can address the issue in future editions.

Working on this book and walking the length and breadth of the Dingle Peninsula has been a pleasure and a privilege. I once thought I knew the peninsula well but it was not until I visited unfamiliar gems like the Great Blasket Island, Clogher Head, The Three Sisters and The Magaharees, for example, that I have really got to know this special peninsula intimately. I sincerely hope you enjoy walking these routes as much as I did and perhaps explore some fresh ones of your own.

So enjoy and let the beauty of the Dingle Peninsula welcome and inspire you.

Using This Book

Maps

The maps in this guidebook are approximate representations of the routes only. For all routes in this guidebook, the use of detailed maps is imperative. All maps listed below are Ordnance Survey Ireland (OSi) Discovery Series 1:50,000 unless otherwise stated. Laminated versions are recommended for durability in wind and rain. Note that 1:50,000 OSi maps do not show cliffs, crags, boulder fields or areas of scree. Also, forestry, tracks and waymarked trails may also change from time to time, so it is useful to get the latest edition. As of 2014, this is the 4th Edition for 1:50,000 maps.

The following 1:50,000 maps are required for this guidebook:

- OSi Sheet 70: **Routes 1–19, 21**
- OSi Sheet 71: **Routes 18–24**

There is also an even more detailed map of the Brandon area and Central Dingle suited for use for Routes 6–17 of this guidebook. Note that this is of a different scale from the 1:50,000 maps and also has different contour intervals and colouring schemes.

- OSi 1:25,000 *Brandon Mountain Weatherproof*, 1st Edition.

Note that an OSi 1:25,000 *Adventure Series* for the Brandon area was proposed in 2014 and may becomes available in later years.

Grid References

Grid references (e.g. **B 928**$_{24}$ **207**$_{72}$) provided in this book should help you plan a route and upload it to your GPS or to use your GPS to check a grid reference on the mountain. Set your GPS to use the Irish Grid (IG). Note that GPS units are precise to 5 digits, whereas a 3-digit precision will usually suffice using map and compass, and hence these are outlined in **bold**.

Walking Times

Walking times in this book are calculated based on individual speeds of 3 to 4km per hour. One minute has also been added for every 10m of ascent, so for example if a height gain of 300m is the case, then 30 minutes would be added to the total walking time. So a 6km route with a total of 300m ascent will take 2 to 2½ hours. In Route 11 (Brandon

Mountain via Paternoster Lakes), I have also added time for the difficulty of terrain.

Note that the 'Time' stated in the routes of this guidebook does **not** include the additional time required for stops, lunch, water intake and photography.

Metric and imperial units are given for road approaches (as some vehicles may be still using miles), total distance, total ascent and mountain heights. However, walking distances are given in metric to conform to OSi maps.

Walk Grades

Walks in this book are graded 1 to 5 based on *level of difficulty*, with 1 being the easiest and 5 the hardest.

None of the routes involves any technical mountaineering or rock climbing. However, note that in winter under snow and ice conditions, all Grade 4 and 5 routes become a serious mountaineering venture requiring the use of winter mountaineering skills, crampons and ice axes. All routes with the exception of Grade 1 walks require three- to four-season hillwalking boots.

Grade 1: Suited for beginners or families with children, these routes are on well-graded or constructed paths with good and firm underfoot conditions. There are little to no navigational difficulties as the routes are generally easy or signposted throughout. Grade 1 routes involve minimal amount of total vertical ascent.

Grade 1/2: Grade 1 routes with over 14km of total distance fall into this category.

Grade 2: Suited for beginners with some hillwalking experience, these routes are generally on formal paths or well-graded, constructed paths with good underfoot conditions. However, there may be some sections of open countryside or slightly rougher ground. The routes are generally signposted, but there may be sections with no signs and require basic navigational skills. Grade 2 routes involve up to 450m of total vertical ascent.

Grade 3: Previous hillwalking experience is required. There may be some formal and signposted paths but generally these routes involve informal paths and rougher ground of open mountainside. There may be some sections of rocky and uneven ground, and small sections of cliffs and moderately steep ground. As they are generally not signed, good navigational skills in all weather conditions are required. Grade 3 routes involve from 400m to 800m of total vertical ascent.

Grade 4:   Suited for those with solid hillwalking experience. Paths are generally informal and underfoot conditions are rough. There may be prolonged sections of rocky and uneven ground. Solid mountain navigation skills are required to cope with all weather conditions. The ability to deal with hazards such as cliffs, small sections of scree and steep ground is required. Grade 4 routes involve from 800m to 1,000m of total vertical ascent.

Grade 5:   Suited for those with solid hillwalking experience. Paths are generally informal and underfoot conditions are rough. There may be prolonged sections of rocky and uneven ground. Solid mountain navigation skills are required to cope with all weather conditions. The ability to deal with hazards such as cliffs, small sections of scree and steep ground is required. There are sections of considerable exposure and where basic scrambling skills are required. Grade 5 routes are strenuous and involve over 1,000m of total vertical ascent.

Access

All land in the Republic of Ireland is owned privately or by the State, with no legal right of entry to the land. When you hear the term 'commonage' it implies that the private property is held in common by a number of joint owners.

Access to upland and mountain areas has traditionally been granted out of goodwill, permission and discretion of the landowners. It is normally good practice to strike up a friendly conversation with a farmer or landowner, and if there is any doubt about access, do ask them. If you are asked to leave, please do so politely and without argument or aggravating the situation.

Note also that the provisions of the Occupiers Liability Act 1995 contain a definition that reduces the landowner's duty of care to hillwalkers. This act contains a category of 'recreational users' who, when they enter farmland, are responsible for their own safety. This has significantly reduced the possibility of successful legal claims against landowners by hillwalkers.

Always use gates and stiles where available. If a gate is closed, close it after entering. If it is open, leave it open. If you cannot open a closed gate to enter, go over at its hinge with care. Take care not to damage any gates, stiles or fences.

When parking, be considerate not to block any gates, farm access lanes or forest entrances as local residents, farm machinery and emergency services may need access at all times.

Note that landowners generally do not approve of dogs being brought on their property, and this includes their land on the open hillside.

Mountain Safety

1. Get a detailed weather forecast. Useful sources of information are www.met.ie, www.mountain-forecast.com and www.yr.no.
2. There is a temperature drop of 2 to 3ºC for every 300m of ascent. If it is a pleasant morning at sea level it could be cold on the summit of Brandon Mountain. The wind is around 25 per cent stronger at 500m than it is at sea level. Wind velocities at a col are higher and wind effects could be strong on an exposed ridge.
3. In case of emergency call 999/112 and ask for 'Mountain Rescue'. Before dialling, it helps to be ready to give a grid location of your position.
4. Keep well away from cliff edges. Be cautious of wet or slippery rock and holes in the ground on vegetated slopes. Take your time traversing a boulder field, descending a scree slope and during scrambling.
5. Rivers, marked as 'thick' blue lines on OSi maps, can sometimes be little streams. Similarly, some streams, marked as 'thin' blue lines, could be wide rivers in reality! Remember also that rivers or streams in flood are dangerous and water levels can rise *very* quickly after or during wet days. Always cross rivers with boots on – remove your socks to keep them dry, use a plastic liner inside your boots to cross, use a towel to dry your feet and boots after, and then put your dry socks back on! Avoid river crossings early in the day. If you cannot cross a river in spate, head upstream to increase your chances in crossing. Do not cross rivers at a bend: rather, cross on a straight.
6. Ensure that you and your clothing and equipment are up to the task, and know the limitations of both. Winter conditions require specialised gear.
7. Be aware of the daylight hours over the time of year. Most accidents happen during descent or near the end of the day. Carry enough emergency equipment (e.g. a head torch, survival shelter and spare batteries) should an injury occur and you need to stop moving.
8. It is recommended not to walk alone, except in areas where there are other people around. Leave word with someone responsible.
9. Do not leave any valuables in cars. Keep all things in the boot and out of sight to avoid unwanted attention.

10. Carry a fully charged mobile phone, but keep it well away from the compass as its needle is affected by metal.
11. Do not solely rely on the use of GPS. Map and compass skills are imperative.
12. Landowners, especially farmers, move their livestock such as cattle from field to field, and up to higher ground, especially in summer. Be wary of bulls in fields and cows that are protecting newborn calves: avoid crossing such fields and go another way. If you find yourself in a field of suddenly wary cattle, do not panic and move away calmly without making any sudden noises. The cows may leave you alone if they think you pose no threat.
13. Keep in mind the deer-rutting season from mid September to end October. Stay well away from stags and deer during this time.

TIP: I recommend the use of a plastic tube about 50cm long, slit into half along its length. This helps crossing barbed-wire fences and also prevents damage to them.

Useful Contacts

Emergencies Dial 999 or 112 for emergency services, including mountain rescue and coastguard.

Weather LoCall 1550 123850 for a detailed five-day Munster forecast using the Met Éireann Weatherdial service.

Maps All walking maps for the Dingle Peninsula may be purchased from www.osi.ie.

Access and Training Mountaineering Ireland, the representative body for walkers and climbers in Ireland, works to secure continued access and to provide walkers and climbers the opportunity to improve their skills. Tel: +353 (0)1 6251115; www.mountaineering.ie

Hillwalking Resource www.mountainviews.ie is a great hillwalking resource and provides mountain lists, comments and information.

Tourist Information For tourist information and information contact the Dingle Tourist Information Office. Tel: +353 (0)66 9151188 or visit www.dingle-peninsula.ie Detailed information on the long distance walking trail of The Dingle Way and other National Waymarked Loops may also be found on www.irishtrails.ie or www.dingleway.com

Transport For intercity train services contact Irish Rail on LoCall 1850 366 222 (or +353 (0)1 8366222 from outside Rep. of Ireland); www.irishrail.ie. For intercity bus services contact Bus Éireann on Tel: +353 (0) 21 4508188 (Cork), +353 (0)64 66 30011 (Killarney), +353 (0)66 7164700 (Tralee), +353 (0)61 474311 (Shannon Airport); www.buseireann.ie.

Great Blasket Island

Experience the rich heritage and magical beauty of Dingle's most beloved island from this powerfully evocative circuit.

Grade:	3
Distance:	9km (5½ miles)
Ascent:	430m (1,411ft)
Time:	3–3¾ hours
Map:	OSi 1:50,000 Sheet 70

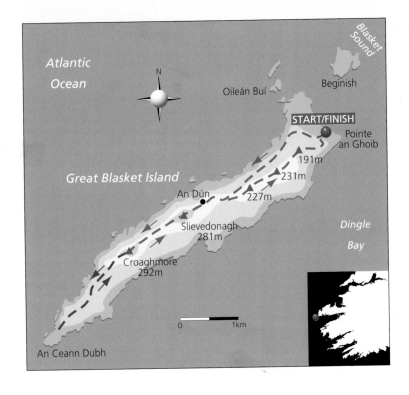

Atlantic Ocean

N

Oileán Buí

Blasket Sound

Beginish

START/FINISH

Pointe an Ghoib

191m

Great Blasket Island

231m

An Dún

227m

Dingle Bay

Slievedonagh 281m

Croaghmore 292m

0   1km

An Ceann Dubh

Start/finish: The landing stage on Great Blasket Island at **V 280**₇₇ **977**₁₁, a few hundred metres north-west of Pointe an Ghoib. Ferries to the island depart from Ventry (*Ceann Tra*) by Blasket Islands Eco Marine Tours (www.marinetours.ie; Tel: +353 (0)86 3353805 or +353 (0)87 2316131), or from Dingle Yacht Marina by Dingle Bay Charters (www.dinglebaycharters.com; Tel: +353 (0)66 9151344 or +353 (0)87 6726100). These typically operate between April and September except in adverse weather conditions. Confirm pick-up times with the skipper of the ferry especially if you plan to stay longer or camp overnight on the island.

The deserted village on the Great Blasket with the sandy cove of An Tráigh Bhán on the left. Sybil Point, Clogher Head and Cruach Mhárthain on the mainland can be seen across Blasket Sound in the distance.

The three ships of the Spanish Armada made no mention of inhabitants on the Great Blasket Island when they passed through Blasket Sound in 1588. The first references of Blasket islanders were made by 18th-century writers who mention families having lived on the island for two or three generations. In 1841, census records listed 153 people living on the island in 28 houses. The numbers dwindled and in 1953 the last 21 islanders were evacuated to Dunquin. The Great Blasket Island, measuring 6km long by 1.2km wide, is the largest of an archipelago of seven islands on the western tip of the Dingle Peninsula. There are several hundred rocks also nearby the islands, with names such as Thunder Rock, Gull Rock and Edge Rocks. This route takes in the entire length of the island, on fine tracks and along its mountainous spine.

Route Description

The rocky slabs at the landing stage may be slippery when wet or when lined with seaweed, so take care and use the chains that are put in place as necessary. Walk up the slabs and around a bend to a platform above the landing stage. Veer left to ascend a grassy ramp between two ruined buildings to reach a T-junction. Take a right here to follow a track gently

The view towards the sea cliffs on the northern side of the Great Blasket and the track that runs above it, with the mainland across Blasket Sound in the distance.

uphill. The track runs above some fields and more ruined buildings. Continue for around 200m to arrive at a fork at **V 278**₂₆ **976**₂₄ just after a house with a yellow door.

The small Irish-speaking community that once lived here, mainly fishermen and farmers, have also left an indelible mark on the literary history of Ireland: *Twenty Years A-Growing* (*Fíche Blian ag Fás*) by Muiris Ó Suilleabháin, *The Islander* (*An t-Oileánach*) by Tomás Ó Criomhthain and *Peig, An Autobiography* (*Peig, Mo Scéal Féin*) by Peig Sayers.

Bear right and follow the track which initially contours along the hillside, passing above some ruined stone cottages of An Baile and the long sandy cove of An Tráigh Bhán, where seals can often be seen basking in the sunshine. The flat islands of Beginish (*Beiginis*, 'small island') and *Oileán na n-Óg* ('island of the young') can also be seen on Blasket Sound. These islands are a breeding ground for hundreds of grey seals in the winter and Arctic terns and seagulls in the summer. Once, a flock of white-fronted Greenland geese over-wintered on the islands.

After a gradual rise the track reaches a flat grassy area where the island of Inishtooskert, shaped like a sleeping giant, comes into view. Our route continues left and south-westward toward Slievedonagh which can now be seen rising ahead. Follow the track, stopping to admire the cliffs and coastal scenery to the right, until reaching the col below Slievedonagh at **V 262**₁₃ **966**₁₅. The junction of grassy tracks here is known locally as 'Traffic Lights'.

Veer right there and follow a firm, narrow path which passes the site of An Dún, an Iron Age promontory fort dating from 800 BC, marked by red circles on the OSi map. All that remains of the fort today are sections of stone wall sinking into the grass. Views north-east along the island and back to the mainland from here are good.

The general direction is now south-west along a path on the grassy and heathery ridge connecting Slievedonagh and Croaghmore, at 292m, the highest point on the island. Keep a lookout for dolphins, porpoises, whales and basking sharks in the waters below. Between Slievedonagh and Croaghmore, note the steep and rocky slopes plummeting down to the sea on the right. Locals call this the 'Fatal Cliff' or 'Sorrowful Slope', where once the Blasket women watched

The path leading to Croaghmore, with Inishvickillane and Tearaght across the sea.

in horror as their men's boats were smashed against the rocks beneath during a gale, drowning them all.

Follow the path as it rises to Slievedonagh, then down a col, before another rise to reach the trig pillar on Croaghmore at **V 246**24 **958**08. The view here is all-encompassing, taking in the nearby islands of Tearaght, Inishnabro and Inishvickillane, further away to the Skelligs and Valentia Island, across to the Iveragh Peninsula before finally looping back to the Dingle mainland.

Inishvickillane, the most southern of the Blasket Islands, is the birthplace of the slow air 'Port na b-Púcaí' or 'faery music'. An Early Christian monastic settlement lies at its south-eastern end. Some families lived on the island in the 19th and 20th centuries. Inishvickillane was bought by the late former Taoiseach Charles Haughey who introduced a herd of native Red Deer to the island.

Inishnabro, an uninhabited island, lies just to the north of Inishvickillane. There is a promontory fort to the south-west of the island and a spectacular rock formation known as Cathedral Rocks to its north-east.

The uninhabited, steep rock pyramid of Tearaght, sitting further north-west from Inishnabro and Inishvickillane, has a dramatically situated lighthouse on its western promontory. First lit on 1 May 1870, it is the most westerly lighthouse in Europe, with a steep funicular railtrack from the landing dock to the lighthouse on top.

An Ceann Dubh Extension

It is possible to continue south-west over a section known locally as the 'Red Ridge' toward the tip of the island, above the precipitous slopes of An Ceann Dubh. Descend to an area of short grass and heather and pass a circular stone enclosure surrounded by sea thrift. Drop into a saddle and continue slightly further until the rocks around An Ceann Dubh are visible. Add 4.5km (3 miles), 240m (787ft) ascent and about 1½–2 hours' walking time for an out-and-back from Croaghmore for this Grade 3 extension.

From Croaghmore, retrace steps along the ridge to Slievedonagh, An Dún and back to Traffic Lights at **V 262**₁₃ **966**₁₅. Ignore tracks at the col and traverse east-north-east along the ridge across points 227m, 231m and 191m. The terrain along the ridge is cushioned with short heather, grass and stag-horn lichen. There a ruins of a signal tower (*Túr Comhartha*), struck by lightning in the 1930s, halfway along at **V 270**₆₄ **970**₀₆. This Napoleonic signal tower is one of several built by the British in the early nineteenth century to warn against the threat of invasion.

Descend the slope beyond the ruins to point 191m, passing a small pile of rocks along the way. At point 191m, veer right along a vague path to regain the track at **V 278**₅₉ **974**₃₀. Turn left and follow the track to reach the fork at the start near the house with the yellow door. Turn right at the fork and descend the way you came, retracing steps to the landing station.

The view northeast from the summit of Croaghmore across the island and towards the mainland.

Mount Eagle and Dunmore Head

Charming country lanes, excellent mountain and coastal views, and the fresh Atlantic air – what more could one ask for?

Grade:	3
Distance:	14.5km (9 miles)
Ascent:	(1,969ft)
Time:	5–6 hours
Map:	OSi 1:50,000 Sheet 70

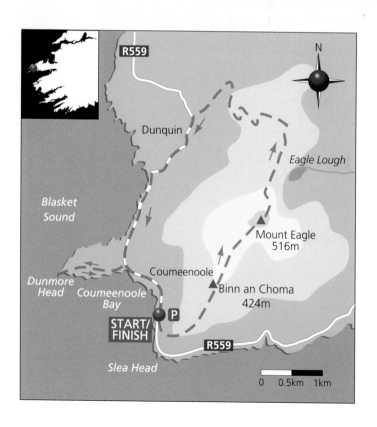

Start/finish: Car park overlooking Coumeenoole Bay along the R559 at **V 317**₈₀ **974**₅₀

Sunset over Great Blasket Island from Dunmore Head, with Inishtooskert to its right.

Mount Eagle (516m/1,693ft), or *Sliabh an Iolair* in Irish, rises above the spectacular coastal road around Slea Head and the beak-like projection of Dunmore Head on the western tip of the peninsula. The hike up to its summit is a perfect introduction to hillwalking on the Dingle Peninsula. The smell of the sea air and the sight of rolling hills is an intoxicating mix. The lower part of the walk takes in charming country lanes and Dunmore Head while the higher section offers magnificent views of Dingle's Atlantic coastline.

Route Description

The car park offers splendid views out to sea and toward Dunmore Head and the cliffs at Carrignaparka. Facing inland, turn right and head south along the R559 toward Slea Head. After 65m or so, there is a grassy ramp leading uphill beyond a metal gate and stile by a Yellow Man signpost. Leave the R559 here and follow the waymarked path, which is part of the Dingle Way, steeply uphill.

After about 600m along the path, the ground starts to level and reaches a cairn sitting atop a boulder. Cross the stile by a stone wall and fence at **V 318**₉₆ **970**₇₂ then turn left immediately to head uphill. Keep the stone wall and fence to your left. The slope is moderately steep and mainly on short grass with the occasional clump of heather and bracken. After a rocky section, the path passes under electric lines and then becomes grassy again.

Pass three stone enclosures after a gap in the wall. Continue to follow the wall upslope, which is intersected by another stone enclosure, until it ends. A firm path then leads uphill through an area of scattered rocks and heather. The slope relents when reaching a cairn at Binn an Choma (point 424m) with a stone circle beneath at **V 327**₇₆ **979**₈₈. Continue uphill beyond the cairn where the stone wall reappears again.

Fabulous sea views open up during the ascent. To the west, a collection of islands adorns the blue waters beyond the broad pointed finger of Dunmore Head. The largest of these is Great Blasket Island, with a scattered group of smaller islands, including Beginish, to its north. Further away still from the Great Blasket are the islands of Inishtooskert, Tearaght, Inishnabro and Inishvickillane. Millennia ago, the high points of the islands once belonged to the same mountain range, instead of being the separate land masses that they are today.

The slope relents closer to the summit and becomes increasingly peaty, with a covering of moor grass and sphagnum moss. Veer north-east to reach the trig-point of Mount Eagle at **V 334**₆₇ **989**₄₇ where sweeping panoramas of land and sea unfold.

Further down the south-east slopes of Mount Eagle lies the townland of Fahan. The hillside here is decorated with clochans – drystone huts in the shape of beehives and thick walls – dating to the early Middle Ages. The ruins of hundreds of these huts prompted one 19th-century antiquarian to call the area the 'city of Fahan'.

Leave the summit and descend north-east to the edge of the plateau at **V 335**₉₆ **990**₉₁ for views of the corrie lake, Eagle Lough. Follow the spur downhill in a northerly direction until reaching a track about 200m away. Continue to descend along the track for just under 1.5km until it bends at **Q 338**₇₅ **004**₂₆. Veer left along the bend as it zigzags down the mountainside to eventually reach a tarmac road. Cruach Mhárthain (403m/1,322ft), rising like a brown pap, dominates the view northwards during the descent.

Turn left at the road and walk down the tarmac to reach a T-junction. Turn left here and continue along the R559, passing the townlands of Glebe and Ballyickeen. The sea is to your immediate right until reaching the land mass of Dunmore Head. At this point, continue along the R559 for around 500m until reaching a narrow tarmac lane to the right at its southern end.

Turn right and walk along this lane for around 250m. Shortly after a car park, leave the tarmac and hop carefully across a fence on the right into a field. Head uphill on the grassy slope using an informal path until reaching a flat grassy area. Pass a ruined building and head westward down the slope for around 200m until the ground starts to fall away steeply into Blasket Sound. There is an ogham stone, an upright stone bearing inscriptions of

The intricate Dingle coastline as seen from high on the western slopes of Mount Eagle.

primitive Irish writing, in the vicinity. The stack of Liúir and some rock slabs can also be seen out to sea. Veer right to descend a steeper slope and continue to its tip at **V301**₅₀ **980**₅₀ to reach the most westernmost point of the Dingle Peninsula and mainland Ireland.

There are fine views of the whaleback hump of Great Blasket Island separated by Blasket Sound. Stop here to reflect on the events that transpired centuries ago on a stormy day in September 1588, when ships of the Spanish Armada sailed through Blasket Sound. Two of the ships managed to get to safety. However, one, the *Santa Maria de la Rosa,* charged out of control through the Sound and collided with other ships. She foundered in the Sound and hundreds of Spanish drowned, including a prince, whose body was eventually laid to rest in an old burial ground in Dunquin.

From here, retrace steps back to the R559 and continue for just over a 1km to reach the car park at Coumeenoole at the start.

ROUTE 3:

Cruach Mhárthain and Clogher Head

Follow in the footsteps of celebrities and a saint in this highly enjoyable walk on the western tip of the Dingle Peninsula.

Grade:	2
Distance:	12.5km (8 miles)
Ascent:	450m (1,477ft)
Time:	4–5 hours
Map:	OSi 1:50,000 Sheet 70

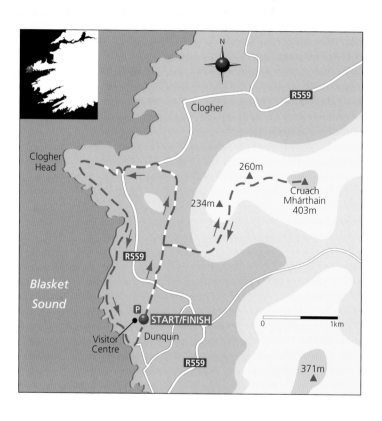

Start/finish: Leave the R559 and turn left at the crossroads by Dunquin Hostel. Continue along the minor road to reach the Blaskets Centre at **Q 315**₁₀ **007**₃₇ and park there.

Fossil-bearing sediments found in Dunquin contain traces of Ireland's volcanic past (*c*. 430 million years ago) which produced ash and rhyolitic lavas. The craggy landforms of Clogher Head are also a testament to the area's volcanic history. This route starts from the

Looking towards Sybil Point and The Three Sisters from the slopes of Cruach Mhárthain.

Blasket Centre and covers a tiny section of the Dingle Way – the 162km (101-mile) long-distance walking trail around the Dingle Peninsula. It follows in the footsteps of filmmakers up to the 403m (1,322ft) summit of Cruach Mhárthain and the headland at Clogher, and passes the holy well of Saint Gobnait. Boasting fabulous mountain and coastal views, this highly enjoyable route is mainly on tarmac and good-quality hill and coastal paths.

Route description

Turn left from the car park and walk back towards the crossroads. Pass the hostel on the right and continue ahead on a narrow lane for around 550m, following Yellow Man signposts. The fuchsia-fringed lane leads uphill, passing some houses before reaching a fork at **Q 317**₇₇ **016**₂₇.

The Dingle Way, signposted by the Yellow Man symbol, veers left here. Do not follow it but instead veer right and take the tarmac lane leading uphill. Continue for a few hundred metres, passing a few houses, before the lane reduces to a broad track beyond a metal gate.

The ascent is gradual and pleasant, with views of Mount Eagle, Dunmore Head and the Blasket Island improving as height is gained. The track eventually reaches the top of a pass between point 234m and point 260m, after the remnants of a cobblestone pavement. This is where the fictional village of Kirrary was built in David Lean's 1970 award-winning film *Ryan's Daughter*. The track then veers right to reach a shoulder to the west of Cruach Mhárthain. Leave the track here at **Q 331**₃₅ **025**₄₀ and veer right on an informal, grassy path toward the summit.

The path is eroded in sections and can be boggy. It steepens beyond an outcrop of rock further upslope. This is an exhilarating section as views toward Sybil Point, Sybil Head and The Three Sisters appear to the left and Clogher Head behind, in addition to that of the Blaskets. The earthen path ascends a moderately steep, heathery slope to reach the grassy summit of Cruach Mhárthain which is marked by a wooden post at a fence corner at **Q 336**₅₂ **024**₇₃.

From the summit retrace steps back to **Q 317**₇₇ **016**₂₇ and

The view toward Mount Eagle, Dunmore Head and Great Blasket Island from the summit of Cruach Mhárthain.

The Dingle Way. Note that the lower slopes west and north of point 234m are heavily farmed and any descent would eventually involve fence- and gate-hopping in addition to crossing fields with livestock – thus making access questionable and therefore best avoided.

Back at **Q 317**₇₇ **016**₂₇, veer right and continue northward along The Dingle Way for about 1km before the track veers left to reaches some houses by the R559. The track is a colourful one in the peak of summer as it is flanked by fuchsia, gorse and heather. On reaching the R559, you may wish to include a short detour by turning right to visit Tig Aine café for refreshments. If not, turn left and walk along the roadside toward Clogher Head.

Leave the R559 after a bend and follow a track on the right toward Clogher Head. This is where director Ron Howard built his set in 1991 for *Far and Away* starring Tom Cruise and Nicole Kidman. After passing below a rocky outcrop on the left, the track gradually rises by some small cairns and then levels off at a larger cairn.

This is an evocative spot where a stunning panorama along the coastline toward Sybil Point and then across to The Three Sisters, Ballydavid Head, Brandon Mountain, Cruach Mhárthain, Mount Eagle and Dunmore Head awaits. The vista goes full circle over islands and sea before arriving back at Sybil Point. The purple-pink and yellow of heather and gorse in the summer add colour to the barren, rocky terrain.

Continue west on the path along the broad summit ridge for around 150m. As soon as the ground starts to drop, veer left at a rocky outcrop and descend south/south-eastward with the sea to your right. A cove appears on the right below after about 1km. Here, veer south/south-west along the coastline. At some stage along this stretch, you will meet signposts for the Siuloid na Cille looped walk. We are still on the film trail and to the left is where the military base set was built for *Ryan's Daughter*.

The signposts lead to a gate with a ladder stile. Cross the stile and follow a green road by some fences. Cross another ladder stile to reach the

Sybil Point, The Three Sisters and Cruach Mhárthain with the Brandon range in the distance from Clogher Head.

ruins of the schoolhouse used in *Ryan's Daughter* at **Q 310**62 **011**79. (Michael Tanner's book *Troubled Epic* tells the warts-and-all story of the fraught film shoot of David Lean's epic). Pass the school on the left to arrive at a signpost near a wall for *Tobar Gobnait* (Gobnait's Well). According to tradition, Saint Gobnait left her native County Clare to escape an enemy. She fled to the Aran Islands (Inis Oírr) where an angel appeared and told her that the 'place of her resurrection' was not there but in a place where she would find nine white deer grazing. Gobnait then left Inis Oírr and travelled along the coast in search of the nine deer. One of the places she visited is Dunquin. Her feast day on 11 February is still celebrated today here.

Ignoring the sign for the well, continue ahead and then right at a fork soon after. The looped walk crosses a grassy field with stiles on both ends, skirts around the coastline, and soon passes the Blasket Centre on the left.

At a corner by a rocky shore with some small rock slabs out to sea, cross a ladder stile and veer left into a field at **Q 313**60 **003**33. Continue to a swinging metal gate which leads to a gravel track of the Dingle Way. Turn left along the track back to the Blasket Centre.

The centre is worth a visit and relates the story of the Great Blasket Island which was evacuated in 1953. It also celebrates the life of the Blasket islanders from the unique literary achievements of its writers, to their culture and tradition.

ROUTE 4:
Sybil Head and The Three Sisters

Explore Dingle's finest sea cliffs on the edge of the Atlantic.

Grade:	3
Distance:	15.5km (9¾ miles)
Ascent:	450m (1,477ft)
Time:	5–6 hours
Map:	OSi 1:50,000 Sheet 70

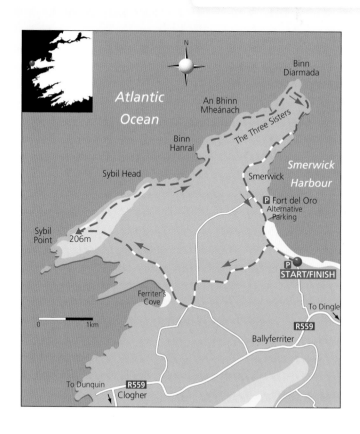

The Dingle Peninsula: A Walking Guide

Start/finish: Coming from Dunquin along the R559, turn left after Ballyferriter town into a boreen signposted 'Smerwick Harbour' and park at the cul-de-sac by the beach at **Q 355**30 **057**60. If you have access to a second car, leave it at Ferriter's Cove B&B if staying there. If not, park near the beach before the B&B or, with permission, at the Sybil Point Golf Course Centre further along the road. By doing so, you will save a few kilometres of road walking at the start.

Ballyferriter (*Baile an Fheirtéarigh*, 'Ferriter's town') is the largest settlement west of Dingle. To the north and east, Smerwick Harbour, a name believed to be Norse in origin, caresses a long stretch of white sandy beaches at Béal Bán, Trá an Fhíona (Wine Strand), Murreagh and Baile na nGall.

Looking through the ruins of the signal tower at Sybil Head toward Sybil Point and Clogher Head, Great Blasket Island and Inishtooskert in the distance.

The waters of Smerwick Harbour are sheltered by a rocky ridge of sea cliffs to the north-west known as The Three Sisters. This ridge stretches further south-west over Sybil Head and down to the dragon-back cliffs of Sybil Point. The coastline boasts some of the finest sea cliffs that the Dingle Peninsula has to offer. A narrow path can be traced along the ridge from Sybil Point to Binn Diarmada, the last of The Three Sisters. The walk starts and ends on Béal Bán beach at Smerwick Harbour.

Route Description

The cliffs at Sybil Head.

From the car park, turn left and walk along the beach. After around 600m, turn left again onto a sandy path between grassy dunes at **Q 350**00 **061**25. The path soon meets a lane that passes through the hamlet of Na Gorta Dubha. Ignore all side-lanes here and continue along the lane to pass the Old Barn Gallery and finally arrive at a T-junction.

Veer left here and continue for 450m to reach another T-junction. Turn right, walk over a concrete bridge and take another right at a fork immediately after. Walk by a small beach on the left followed by some holiday homes, before passing Ferriter's Cove B&B. Arrive at a T-junction shortly after and take a left here onto a narrow lane. (Note that a right here leads to the Sybil Point Golf Course Centre.)

Just after a bend by a house on the left, the lane diverges at **Q 328**₀₀ **057**₄₅ and forms a small circle around a group of farmhouses. Take a left at the fork and continue in a semicircle to reach a junction. Turn left here and follow a dirt road uphill flanked by houses. After the last house on the left, the road changes to a broad track bordered by fields.

Follow the track uphill to reach a fork at **Q 323**₄₀ **060**₄₂. Turn left there, ignore the first metal gate on the right and continue for a few metres to reach a set of metal gates, one ahead and another to its right. Go through the metal gate on the right and ascend the dirt track uphill. An electric fence edges a field on the left. A deep ditch separates the track from a fenced field to the right.

Further to the south-west is Caisleán an Fheirtéaraigh (Ferriter's Castle), situated above a small cove near Ceann an Dúna. The castle once belonged to Piaras Feiritear, an Irish poet and harpist who fought in the siege of Tralee in 1641. After the fall of Ross Castle in 1652, he was captured by Colonel Nelson's men in Castledrum and hanged.

You are now heading up the slopes of Ballyoughtereagh (An Baile Uachtarach, 'the upper townland'). The track bends left a few hundred metres uphill, then veers right a few metres further on to cross a ditch at **Q 319**₆₉ **061**₂₆. Cross the electric fence with care after the ditch, then go uphill, keeping the fence to your right. (Note: there is another fence farther left of the field, separated by a grassy ditch).

Ascend the grassy slope, which is peppered with thistles and weeds. Just over a hundred metres uphill go through a gap in the electric fence and veer left. Walk a few metres across a grassy field to reach a grassy ditch, bordered by an electric fence. Head uphill, keeping the electric fence and ditch to your left.

The ditch soon veers left higher up the slope. Keep following the fence uphill and pass a rocky mound along the way. Cross the electric fence below the clifftop then follow a narrow path flanked by bracken to reach the top of the ridge overlooking the sea. At the top, bear left on a narrow grassy path toward the signal tower (marked on the OSi map as Túr Comhartha) above Sybil Point at **Q 314**₅₅ **063**₁₆.

The tower, within sight of the ones on Great Blasket Island and Ballydavid Head, was built by the British in the late 18th century to guard against an impending Napoleonic attack. Keep a safe distance from the precipitous 200m/656ft-high cliffs at all times and do not veer off the path. The view is stunning, with the switchback line of The Three Sisters

Coastline and cliffs along the path leading to Binn Diarmada, one of the Three Sisters.

to the north-east and Brandon Mountain as the backdrop. In the opposite direction, the Blasket Islands can be seen.

Retrace steps from the tower to the point where you topped out on the cliff. From here, continue along the clifftop of Sybil Head. Follow a narrow path wherever possible on the seaward side, keeping a fence to your right. The point and head were named after Sybil Lynch, native of County Galway. She eloped with one of the Feiritears and was pursued by her father. She took refuge in a sea cave nearby while her father bombarded Caisleán an Fheirtéaraigh. When the battle ended, her father's men discovered that the tide had swept through the sea cave and washed her away.

A narrow path flanked by bracken, heather and gorse weaves along the airy clifftop. Cross a fence before descending into a dip. This is followed by a slight rise to reach a stone enclosure at **Q 326**08 **070**99 where views of sea cliffs back to the tower are good.

From the enclosure, cross a fence then descend to its corner, where a rocky bay and the first of The Three Sisters – Binn Hanraí – come into view. Continue along a grassy field close to the clifftop to reach a fence at **Q 331**36 **071**40. Follow the fence by keeping it to your right and cross all fences that bisect it. Leave the fence at a corner and veer left to ascend a narrow path flanked by heather, gorse and bracken to reach the top of Binn Hanraí.

A path flanked by overgrown bracken with a fence to its right leads away from the summit. The path dips and rises to the next of The Three Sisters – An Bhinn Mheánach. It follows close to a stone wall and fence initially before leaving it to reach the top of An Bhinn Mheánach, where views are stunning.

Descend from the top, following a fence. Cross the fence where it intersects with another near a pile of rocks and descend a gentle, grassy slope. Later, veer left for a stiff pull up to the last of The Three Sisters – Binn Diarmada. The steep slope is initially on short grass, but later there are large rock slabs and vertiginous cliffs on the seaward side and the ground underfoot is dominated by heather and bracken. The top, splashed with clusters of pink seathrift, is a precipitous ledge marked by a sharp, rocky fin.

The ledge is said to be where the legendary Diarmuid and Gráinne slept while being pursued by the Fianna. It was here also that Europe first greeted the navigator Charles Lindberg who in 1927 flew the first solo transatlantic flight from New York to Paris in *The Spirit of St Louis*. He signalled a fishing vessel and continued towards Valentia Island, where news of his arrival was announced by the radio station to the world.

The view from Binn Diarmada back to Sybil Head and across Smerwick Harbour to Ballydavid Head and Brandon Mountain is stunning. Descend south/south-eastward down a steep slope of short grass to reach a stone enclosure at **Q 353**₇₇ **087**₄₄. From here, veer left to descend a grassy slope toward the cliff edge ahead. There is a sea cove under the dark cliffs of Binn Diarmada, which now looms above. With Smerwick Harbour on the left, follow a path by the clifftop to reach a metal gate at **Q 353**₈₇ **080**₉₄.

Follow the track beyond the gate, which is flanked by fields with livestock, to reach a tarmac road. Continue on the road, passing houses, farm buildings and a junction on the right. Ignore the junction and continue ahead to pass a junction on the left signposted 'Fort del Oro' (*Dún an Óir*, 'fortress of the gold') and pointing towards Ard na Caithne ('height of the arbutus') harbour.

Beach at Ballyferriter, with Binn Diarmada on the left and Ballydavid Head and the Brandon range to the right.

In 1578, the English seaman Martin Frobisher sent 11 ships home laden with what he thought was gold ore from Baffin Island. One ship containing 110 tonnes crashed at the waters of Ard na Caithne. When it was discovered that the stone – a dark igneous rock – was not gold, it was used to build a fort. Two years later in 1580, at a strand near the fort, 600 Irish, Italian and Spanish men and women were massacred by the Crown forces led by General Arthur Grey during the Desmond Rebellion. Some of them were decapitated, their corpses thrown into the sea and their heads buried in a field called Gort na gCeann, or 'Field of the heads'. You may wish to take detour at the junction toward a cul-de-sac to visit the site of the fort, of which little remains today. A stone monument with twelve heads stands there.

If not, continue ahead to the end of the road, pass some houses and reach Béal Bán beach once again. Walk along the beach for around 1km back to the start.

Ballydavid Head and Beenmore

This short walk provides breathtaking views of sea cliffs, sea coves and the Brandon massif.

Grade:	3
Distance:	8km (5 miles)
Ascent:	400m (1,312ft)
Time:	2¾–3¼ hours
Map:	OSi 1:50,000 Sheet 70

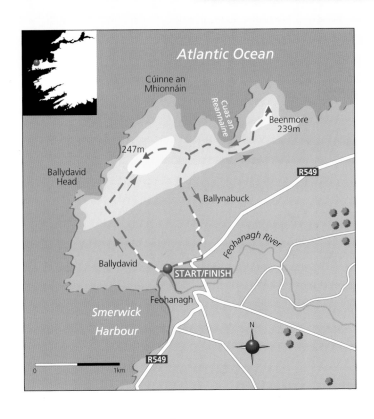

Start/finish: At **Q 390**₈₁ **100**₇₄, on a gravel patch at the lay-by to the left of a minor road just after Feohanagh village. Alternative parking spaces are available at Feohanagh village on the R549.

The view southwest from Ballydavid Head across Smerwick Harbour toward Mount Eagle, Cruach Mhárthain and The Three Sisters.

Dinnseanchas, or place-lore, is important in Irish culture as it translates the geographical element of the Celtic landscape into a rich narrative. Every summit, cliff, valley, lake, cove, sea inlet, island and townland in Ireland has its own story and secrets woven into the fabric of its place name. Ballydavid, known locally as Baile na nGall or 'town of the foreigner', has its share of *dinnseanchas* too. Its nearby harbour, Smerwick, was a hub of a seventh-century Christian community until the Vikings arrived. The name Smerwick is derived from the Norse words *smoer* and *wik*, meaning 'butter' and 'harbour'. It was from the Viking settlements here that butter was shipped to Limerick. History also records a Papal convoy of 600 Spanish, Italian and Basque soldiers who landed in 1580, who were later massacred by the English forces led by Admiral Winter, Ormonde and Earl Grey. This route goes a step further away from its lonely byroads and explores the magnificent line of sea cliffs at Ballydavid Head from above An Caisleán ('the Castle') to the airy perch of Beenmore (239m/784ft). Keep a safe distance from the edge of the cliffs at all times!

Route Description

The route starts and ends in a quiet corner of Feohanagh. The name (in Irish, *An Fheothanach*) comes from an old Irish word for 'a windy place'.

Turn left at the lay-by and walk uphill along the byroad, passing some houses. Ignore a junction to the right and continue until reaching a fork by the last two houses on the road. Take a left at the fork and follow a track to reach a metal gate. Go through the gate and arrive at a set of three metal gates soon after at **Q 384**₃₆ **104**₅₀.

Looking toward Beenmore, Beennaman, Masa-tiompan and the Brandon range in cloud from the ruins of the signal tower at Ballydavid Head.

There are two metal gates to the right, and one on the left. Go through the one on the left and follow a grassy path uphill with a stone wall and fence on your right. When the fence and wall end, continue uphill on a grassy slope with patches of heather and gorse until reaching the clifftop. The best views are from the clifftop above An Caisleán where you can look down on the cliffs and rock stacks below and across Smerwick Harbour toward The Three Sisters.

With the sea to your left, ascend a gentle slope to reach the ruins of a large signal tower at point 247m at **Q 387**₄₆ **113**₀₃. Built during Napoleonic times, the ruined tower is perched close to a rib of rock along a moderately narrow ridge. Continue north-eastward along the ridge for a few hundred metres from the signal tower, passing large rock slabs and the remnants of an old wall.

At the end of the ridge above Cúinne an Mhionnáin, descend south-eastward on a grassy slope to reach a fence at **Q 391**₉₆ **113**₅₅. Cross a further two fences before descending to a dip on a path flanked by overgrown bracken, heather and gorse. The impressive 250m-wide sea cove of Cuas an Reannaine lies at the bottom of precipitous sea cliffs to the left.

Along the clifftop path toward Beenmore above the sea cove at Cuas an Reannaine.

These massive cliffs act as rocky bulwarks against the fierce Atlantic waves. Beenmore can be seen rising impressively ahead.

Cross a fence at the dip, then follow another line of fences. There is a narrow path to the left of the fence, on the seaward end. Take care during this stretch as the path traverses relatively close to the cliff edge in places.

The view across Cuas an Reannaine toward Pointe an Ghiorria, Cúinne an Mhionnáin and Ballydavid Head from the summit of Beenmore.

Veer north-east and away from the fence for a stiff pull up to Beenmore. The summit is an airy perch on a narrow strip of grass graced with heather and bracken at **Q 401**₆₈ **118**₁₉. Enjoy superb views back toward Ballydavid Head, with Eagle Mountain, Cruach Mhárthain and The Three Sisters rising beyond. In the other direction, Masatiompan can be seen across Brandon Creek, with Brandon Mountain to its right.

Retrace steps from the summit back to at **Q 391**₉₆ **113**₅₅. Veer left here and descend the slope using an intermittent sheep's path toward a metal gate at **Q 391**₄₃ **109**₃₁. Go through the gate and follow the track downhill to a pair of metal gates. Bypass these carefully on the left and continue on the track as it soon improves to become a tarmac lane.

Pass some houses and a farm building and continue to a T-junction by the R549. Turn right and continue along the R549 for around 200m. Leave it at a bend and follow the byroad ahead back to the start.

Sunset over Ballydavid Head from Dooneen Pier.

Reenconnell

This modest gem of a hill offers a spectacular panorama of Brandon Mountain and Dingle West.

Grade:	1
Distance:	3.5km (2¼ miles)
Ascent:	205m (673ft)
Time:	1–1½ hours
Map:	OSi 1:50,000 Sheet 70 or OSi 1:25,000 *Brandon Mountain*

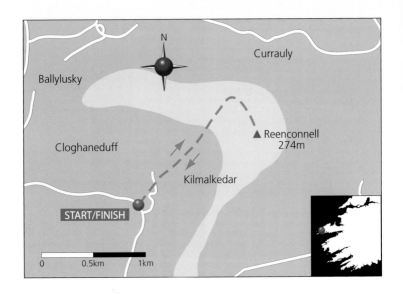

Start/Finish: Along a laneway by Kilmalkedar church and graveyard at **Q 402**03 **061**90.

The glorious panorama of Mount Eagle, Cruach Mhárthain and Smerwick Harbour, looking west from Reenconnell's broad summit ridge.

The hill of Reenconnell (274m/899ft) rises above the townland of Kilmalkedar in the western end of the Dingle Peninsula, east of Murreagh. For its modest height, its grassy summit ridge gives wonderful views of the entire Brandon range to the east and a panorama of rolling hills and the sea to the west. This is the easiest walk of the entire Dingle Peninsula in this guidebook. It is suitable as a simple hike for beginners or a family with children, or as a short, romantic stroll to admire the sunrise or sunset.

Route Description

Kilmalkedar is an ancient church site on the Dingle Peninsula probably founded by St Maolcethair in the seventh century. The present church, however, was built in the mid 12th century and displays an architecture essentially Irish Romanesque in style, with its chevrons and diamond shapes. There is a sixth-century standing stone inside the church carved with the Latin alphabet, a small cross and the letters 'DNI'. Outside the church is a graveyard; its front section has an early sundial, a large stone cross and an ogham stone. An ogham stone is a standing stone with a series of slashes carved across its edge. Many are found scattered around the entire Dingle Peninsula.

From the start point near the church, walk north-east along the lane with the graveyard on the right, then follow a yellow 'Saint' signpost up a stony track that eventually bends left at a metal gate. Shortly after, there is a sliding metal gate on the right. Go through this gate, continue to follow the signposts and enter a green field at **Q 403**27 **063**07 which is normally full of sheep. This route is part of the *Cosán na Naomh*, or 'the road of the Saints', a 18km/11-mile pilgrim route that links the ancient Christian sites on the Dingle Peninsula. At the far end of the field, there is a ladder stile

41

Kilmalkedar church and graveyard.

at **Q 404**₇₈ **064**₄₄ that leads to another field with stone walls on either side. Climb over this stile and then immediately veer left to surmount yet another ladder stile that provides access to the next field.

Once in this field, continue on uphill, keeping the wall and fence on the right, to eventually reach a ladder stile and a metal gate. The ascent is a gradual one beyond this on a grassy path flanked by clumps of compact rush, gorse patches and by a wall on its far right. Walk uphill for a distance of about 400m and come to another ladder stile and a metal gate at **Q 407**₁₈ **066**₈₅. The wall on the right is now heavily covered in heather and gorse. Keep following the yellow-marked signposts to the col where there is a step stile at **Q 411**₄₆ **071**₂₅.

Bear right here, with a stone wall also on the right, in a general south-east direction. After about 300m, the wall intersects a fence corner at **Q 413**₀₅ **069**₀₉. Get over it carefully without damaging the wall, using wooden posts to maintain balance. If unable to, then go no further, as the views from here are no different from those at the summit. However, if you do, then walk a short distance away beyond the wall to the highest point of Reenconnell at **Q 413**₂₆ **068**₀₀.

The view from the col and all along the grassy ridge toward the summit of Reenconnell is all encompassing – a priceless gem. I fondly recall how much it took me by surprise during my first wander to these heights some years back. The entire Brandon range, from Masatiompan (763m/2,503ft) to Ballysitteragh (623m/2,044ft), sweeps the view to the east. To the west, gentle hills – Mount Eagle (516m/1,693ft) to the far left and the pointed Cruach Mhárthain (403m/1,322ft) to its right – rise beyond the broad arm of Smerwick Harbour and the rolling landscape of the peninsula.

After enjoying the views and perhaps also a picnic or an embrace or both, retrace steps back to Kilmalkedar and the start point of the walk.

The southern end of Smerwick Harbour and the brown pap of Cruach Mhárthain rising beyond dominate the view west from the col near Reenconnell.

Piaras Mór and Masatiompan

Enjoy an ascent of two mountains on the edge of the sea with grand views, especially at sunset.

Grade:	3
Distance:	10km (6¼ miles)
Ascent:	800m (2,625ft)
Time:	3¾–4¾ hours
Map:	OSi 1:50,000 Sheet 70 or OSi 1:25,000 *Brandon Mountain*

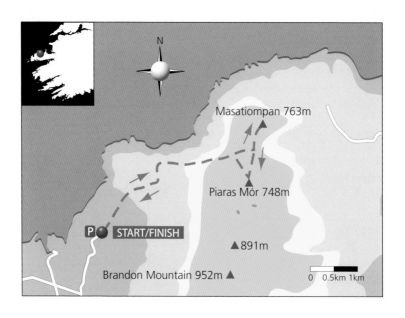

Start/finish: Large car park at a cul-de-sac at **Q 433**₆₈ **124**₆₈ north of Ballinknockane, off the R549.

At the edge of the Atlantic on the Dingle Peninsula is a mountain that rises like a sentinel above the sea. This peak, Masatiompan (763m/2,503ft), marks the start of the mighty ridge that extends southward, over Piaras Mór (748m/2,454ft), and then

Looking eastwards along the spur leading to Cnoc na mBristí and the steep mountainside that soars from the sea to the summit of Masatiompan above.

toward a mountain massif named after St Brendan, a fifth-to-sixth-century monastic saint. This walk is a fine mix of mountains and sea, and serves as the perfect introduction to the Brandon group of hills. Its location by the sea also makes Masatiompan a fine high-level viewpoint to savour an Atlantic sunset from the heights of the Dingle Peninsula.

Route Description

The car park at the start of the walk overlooks Brandon Creek where St Brendan set sail in a small leather curragh with a band of pilgrims to seek out the Promised Land in the sixth century. From the car park, head north-east, going through a metal gate. Walk along a stony track, following Yellow Man signposts and pass a further two metal gates. After the second metal gate at **Q 444**₆₅ **135**₇₉, bear left, to eventually pass an area of turf-cutting.

Now ascend the slopes northward to a peaty col where a plunging view of the sea and cliffs suddenly reveals itself overlooking a fence. The spur leading to Cnoc na mBristí lies ahead, and beyond that is the steep mountainside that rises from the sea at Brandon Head to the summit of Masatiompan.

While ascending the moderate grassy slopes

Looking down onto Beennaman, Brandon Creek and Beenmore from Cnoc na mBristí.

up the spur, look toward the brownish-green landscape due south. It is said that once a community of monks lived and farmed in fields around here, so much so that the area is locally known as Fothar na Manach or 'field of the monks'. Continue along until nearing the top of the spur below some rocky outcrops. Cross a fence at its corner (**Q 449**44 **138**22) beside a small 'fang' of rock in order to gain this top, where there are fine views back down to Beennaman (378m/1,240ft), Brandon Creek and Smerwick Harbour. Beyond this, the slope relents and eventually reaches a metal gate and the Yellow Man sign at **Q 453**62 **138**44.

Go through the gate and keep following the track, part of The Dingle Way, that rises gradually to the col at **Q 464**90 **141**20. A band of dark-grey rock guards Masatiompan's south-west slopes above on the left as you near the col. On reaching the col, you may want to wander on the opposite side of the fence where there is an ogham stone bearing an inscription. Returning to the col, keep the fence on the right and ascend a rocky and mossy slope following the fence until reaching a small pile of rocks with a standing stone on the summit of Masatiompan at **Q 465**36 **145**48.

On all my visits here over the years, the fence has been damaged on the summit slopes, perhaps by the elements. Take a short detour and descend north-east, beyond a step stile to reach a Red Man marker at the edge of a slope at **Q 465**88 **145**98 before it starts to fall steeply down the mountainside. You are now standing on slopes high above Brandon Head, and the view eastward here is breathtaking. The arc of Sauce Creek, a deep sheltered cove, can be seen poking inland just beyond it. Steep mountainside that rises above Sauce Creek and its brownish upper slopes extends eastward to Brandon Point. The curved arm of Brandon Bay lies further still with the mountains of the eastern end of the Dingle Peninsula inland.

Retrace steps back to the summit of Masatiompan, and then descend back to the col. From the col, ascend in a general southerly direction to pass a ring fort, and later gain the summit of Piaras Mór at **Q 463**81 **136**52, which is marked by a small cairn on jumble of rocky outcrops. There are views of Brandon Mountain and the Faha ridge to the south, and views back toward Masatiompan northward are quite good.

Leave the summit of Piaras Mór and walk down grassy slopes to re-emerge on the track at **Q 460**33 **140**57, following Yellow Man signs back to the start point and passing six metal gates along the way.

Sauce Creek from Brandon Point

Let the fresh Atlantic breezes invigorate you and the barren landscape mystify you en route to a dramatic coastal feature.

Grade:	3
Distance:	13.5km (8½ miles)
Ascent:	430m (1,411ft)
Time:	4¼–5¼ hours
Map:	OSi 1:50,000 Sheet 70 or OSi 1:25,000 *Brandon Mountain*

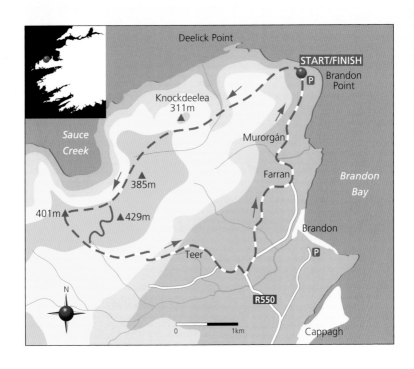

Start/finish: Car park at the end of the R550 at Brandon Point (**Q 526**₁₅ **172**₇₄).

Metal gate and stile along the Siuloid a' tSais footpath above Brandon Point with Brandon Bay and the mountains beyond in the distance.

Brandon Point is a popular spot for birdwatchers. In the autumn, the Great Skua and Manx Shearwater are frequent visitors. In early winter, it is the turn of the guillemot and razorbill. According to eighth-century folklore, it was here that the legendary Bran mac Febail and his men landed after sailing in the Other World and spending what they thought was only a year in the magical Land of Women. They had of course been away much longer. When one of his men, Nechtan mac Collbran, set foot on the shore at Brandon Point, he turned to ashes. Brandon Point, or Srón Bhroin, is also a good vantage point to appreciate the wide sweep of land across Brandon Bay from its flat tip at Tonaranna to the hills dominated by Beenoskee farther south. The area between Brandon Point and Masatiompan is a desolate stretch of wild moorland bounded to the Atlantic by precipitous cliffs. The most interesting and dramatic feature is Sauce Creek, a large U-shaped sea inlet with 400m/1,312ft-high steep scree-strewn slopes. This route follows the trail of the waymarked *Siulóid a' tSais* route to the clifftop of Sauce Creek, then from there back along a lonely mountain road to Teer (An Tír) and toward Farran (An Fearann), Murorgán and Brandon Point.

Route Description

Cross the stile at the car park and ascend the path on the grassy slope westward, keeping the fence and sea on your right. The path becomes stony beyond a metal gate and stile, rising to reach the *Siulóid a' tSais* signpost at **Q 517**₇₁ **168**₇₉.

After crossing a level area, the signposts lead downhill to reach a stream. This is a lush, green hollow surrounded by a set of green hillocks. Cross the stream and follow the signposts as the path gradually rises to a flat area overlooking the sea below the slopes of Knockdeelea. Rock pipits, meadow pipits, black-backed gulls, choughs, kittiwakes and stonechats grace the skies and breathe life to this brown moorland of desolate wilderness.

Sauce Creek from near Slieveglass, with Masatiompan and the Brandon range in cloud beyond.

Follow the path as it undulates and then rises to a cliff edge overlooking Sauce Creek at **Q 497**₂₂ **157**₉₇. Sauce Creek is a large U-shaped sea inlet, measuring nearly 700m from end to end, and nearly 1km from the sea. Its flanks are guarded by steep scree slopes and precipitous cliffs plunging from the clifftop. For the best views down the Creek, cross the fence and walk a few metres to the clifftop but keep a safe distance from its edge. There is an impressive backdrop of Masatiompan and Brandon Mountain beyond Sauce Creek.

Anglicisation has made Sauce Creek lose its meaning. The Irish word *sás* or *Sais* means 'noose trap'. Easy to see why, the way the Creek is shaped and with its steep cliffs. Local fisherman will tell you that 'anything that goes in there won't come out'. It was not so long ago in the last century that three families lived down in its inhospitable depths. One of those families even remained into the early years of this century.

With Sauce Creek to the right, follow the path along the clifftop to reach a fence with a stile near point 401m at **Q 487**₈₅ **150**₉₆. Cross the stile and continue a short distance to point 401m, where one can see many mountains of Dingle West, dominated by the sprawling mass of Brandon Mountain closer at hand.

Short/point 429m variation

It is possible to reduce the route length at the clifftop above Sauce Creek by turning left midway at **Q 494**70 **152**10 following the *Siulóid a' tSais* signpost. The path leads downhill and meets up with The Dingle Way track. For keen summit baggers, veer left after around 200m downhill for the short ascent to Point 429, known as *Faill an tSáis* hill by www.mountainviews.ie.

Cross the stile again at point 401m. Descend by initially following a fence on the right, then veer left and away from it to meet a path downhill at **Q 489**92 **145**61. The path meets a track around 100m away. Turn left at the track and follow Yellow Man signposts to reach a metal gate with a turnstile around 2.5km away at **Q 508**11 **145**77.

The track eventually becomes a lane which meanders downhill toward Teer, passing the Tees Gallery, to meet the R550. Ignore all side-lanes until meeting the R550. Turn left on the R550 and walk towards Brandon Point.

After around 350m, leave the R550 to take a left at the fork following Yellow and Red Man signposts along a lane which meanders uphill but later descends to the hamlet of Farran. Turn left at Farran and continue for around 2km along the R550 back to the start.

Sauce Creek.

Brandon Mountain from the East

An evocative circuit along one of the finest mountain ridges in Ireland.

Grade:	4
Distance:	10km (6¼ miles), based on Start/Finish grid locations given.
Ascent:	980m (3,215ft)
Time:	4–5 hours
Map:	OSi 1:50,000 Sheet 70 or OSi 1:25,000 *Brandon Mountain*

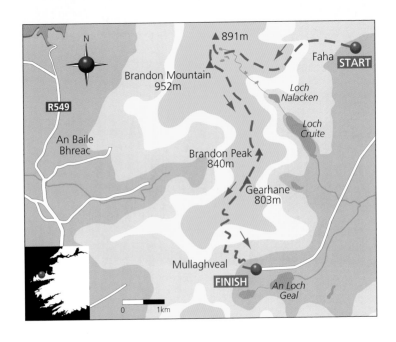

START: The car park at a cul-de-sac (**Q 493**₈₂ **119**₆₂) at Faha, a townland on slopes above the village of Cloghane.

FINISH: Leave a second car at around **Q 470**₅₀ **069**₀₀ or parked somewhere along the road marked as The Pilgrim's Route on the OSi map. Otherwise, it is a long walk on tarmac (about 8km/5miles) back to the car park at Faha, adding a further 2–2¾ hours to the total time.

The view northwards back to Brandon Mountain from its summit ridge. The Faha ridge extends to the right in the distance.

Brandon Mountain (952m/3,123ft) or Cnoc Bréanainn is one of my favourite Irish summits. It is the highest point in Ireland outside the chain of peaks that dominate the MacGillycuddy's Reeks. There is an unearthly quality – powerful and uplifting – on its lofty heights, and in particular along its ridge, which takes in two other summits: Brandon Peak (840m/2,756ft) and Gearhane (803m/2,634ft). It is common for this mountain range to 'wear its cap' on cloudy days, but on a clear day, views of mountain, lake, land and sea from its summit ridge are unparalleled. This route approaches the mighty Brandon from its more interesting eastern side at Faha.

Route Description

A signboard for 'Going Climbing?' and 'The Country Code' catches the eye at the car park. Walk to a metal gate, passing the signs for 'Mt Brandon' and the Yellow Man. Go through a wooden gate and up a grassy ramp toward the Grotto, crossing a metal ladder stile and a small metal gate on the way. Walk along a stony path with patches of gorse, passing just under the

Grotto. Cross some wooden step stiles, following white metal posts, then walk through a gap in the fence. Continue this uphill progress on the path until just below the Faha ridge at **Q 481**$_{74}$ **120**$_{36}$. An airplane, the *Condor*, belly-landed on top of the Faha Ridge in 1940: four crew members suffered broken limbs while two emerged unscathed. Another aircraft, carrying six Polish crew involved in hunting U-boats, crashed and exploded on the slopes of Brandon Mountain in 1943.

Contour along under the slopes of Faha, following the path until the white posts end around **Q 476**$_{12}$ **114**$_{85}$. The coniferous plantation indicated here on the OSi map no longer exists. There are splashes of yellow paint dabbed on rock that marks the path ahead, and it becomes littered with boulders.

The path becomes firmer underfoot as it bends inward around **Q 470**$_{70}$ **115**$_{52}$, winding its way under the rocky sandstone crags of the mighty Faha ridge towering above. In the valley below on the left, the paternoster lakes come into sight, a series of lakes under the steep eastern side of the Brandon range strung together like rosary beads, the largest of which is Loch Cruite ('Harp Lake'), followed by Loch Nalacken ('Duck Lake'), and then a group of smaller lakes nestled in rocky shelves leading up the valley. It is a lovely setting.

In the mist, the following grid locations will be helpful as you enter the boulder-filled amphitheatre of a bare rocky glen of sheer walls and scree slopes: **Q 465**$_{04}$ **118**$_{52}$ (there is a yellow arrow on rock) and **Q 463**$_{45}$ **118**$_{14}$ (there is yellow paint on rock). From here, walk south of a small tarn to the bottom of a headwall at **Q 461**$_{65}$ **118**$_{32}$. The path swings right here up a very steep (the use of hands may be required) but straightforward gully leading to a col at the top of the ridge (**Q 460**$_{58}$ **120**$_{45}$).

Once you top out, a striking vision of mountain and the sea greets you. Continue left (south) up a moderate slope leading to the summit of Brandon Mountain at **Q 460**$_{46}$ **116**$_{05}$ with its cairn, trig point, fence posts and a cross on a pile of rock. The remains of St Brendan's Oratory and a holy well are also said to mark the summit.

The view from Brandon Mountain is a dreamland of mountain panoramas: the imposing Faha ridge close at hand; the majestic line of mountain running north to south; the intricate coastline west with views of Smerwick Harbour, The Three Sisters, Great Blasket Island and a scattering of other islands; the curved arc of Brandon Bay to the east and the mountains of the rest of the peninsula; and lovely valleys and moorland to the west.

The next 3km or so are an exhilarating ridge walk. The ridge snakes south-east like a prehistoric reptile with sharp, angular fins; its eastern end plunges into the depths of the paternoster lakes like a yawning abyss. Staying a safe distance away from this sharp end, descend in a south-east direction to meet a wall, fence post and a path that later crosses the wall at

Q 463₆₇ **113**₁₄. Continue on the ridge south-east, and then south, leaving it only at around **Q 470**₀₀ **096**₀₀ for a stiff pull up to the summit of Brandon Peak: on its top look back along the ridge you traversed. After savouring this and other views from the fang-shaped summit, which are just as good as from Brandon Mountain, descend south-west, with the grassy ridge narrowing just before the top of Gearhane. Continue on: there is a Green Man sign at **Q 468**₂₄ **087**₇₃ on southern slopes below Gearhane marking St Brendan's way, along with a gate and a fence.

Descend downhill on moorland to meet a track at **Q 463**₅₄ **081**₂₀. Turn left once on the track, following a series of zigzags down into the valley of Mullaghveal, with the small lake of Loch na mBan visible in the distance on the right during the descent. A green road is reached and this eventually passes a ruined stone-walled dwelling on the right. The track meanders on near a stream on the left, and zigzags down to meet a metal gate at **Q 467**₈₃ **069**₁₆. Here, turn left onto a main track that leads to the finish at **Q 470**₅₀ **069**₀₀.

The Paternoster Lakes, the eastern end of the Faha ridge, Brandon Bay and the eastern hills of the Dingle Peninsula as seen from Brandon Mountain.

Brandon Mountain from the West

An easier route to the summit of one of Ireland's most iconic mountains.

Normal Route	
Grade:	3
Distance:	7km (4¼ miles)
Ascent:	780m (2,559ft)
Time:	3–3¾ hours
Map:	OSi 1:50,000 Sheet 70 or OSi 1:25,000 Brandon Mountain

Brandon Ridge Variation	
Grade:	4
Distance:	19km (11¾ miles)
Ascent:	950m (3,117ft)
Time:	6½–8 hours
Map:	OSi 1:50,000 Sheet 70 or OSi 1:25,000 Brandon Mountain

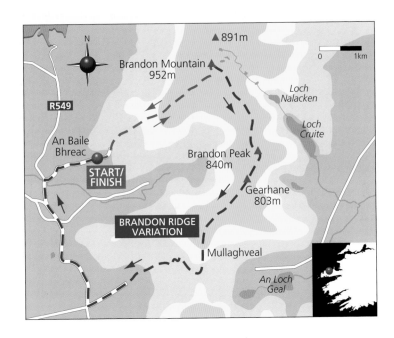

Start/Finish: A large car park at **Q 433**₉₀ **094**₃₃ at the end of a cul-de-sac signposted 'Mt Brandon' on the western side of the mountain in An Baile Breac, off the R549.

Looking southeast from the slopes of Brandon Mountain to the magnificent fang-like ridge that extends to Brandon Peak.

The 'Path of the Saints' or *Cosán na Naomh* is an old pilgrimage road from Dingle to the foot of Brandon Mountain via Ventry, An Riasc and Kilmalkedar Church. Around 18km (11 miles) in length, it connects many of the early Christian sites on the Dingle Peninsula. An extension of the Cosán na Naomh now culminates on the summit of Brandon Mountain (952m/3,123ft). The summit is known to be the site where Saint Brendan meditated in the sixth century before leaving on his epic voyage to Greenland and America. It was on these slopes where he reportedly ousted the pagan deity Crom Dubh. From being the site of Celtic harvest celebrations and known by the name Sliabh Daidche, the mountain was to be forever seen in a different light by post-pagan Ireland. This route follows the signposts of *Cosán na Naomh* to the summit of Brandon Mountain from its gentler western side via the Stations of the Cross. A variation is provided for those intending to continue along the Brandon ridge.

Route Description

A board at the car park describes the *Cosán na Naomh* (Path of the Saints), an old pilgrimage road linked with St Brendan. There is also a new stone memorial dedicated to 'people who followed in the path of St Brendan for the cure of cancer' at the car park. The route to the summit of Brandon Mountain is signposted throughout.

At the end of the car park, cross the bridge over the stream and follow the track uphill with the river now on the left until reaching a metal gate with a swinging metal gate on its right. Go through this and continue on for a distance of 100m or so until **Q 437**20 **096**47. At this point, veer left away from the green track and follow wooden (white) posts, crossing a stream to a pile of rocks with a wooden cross in the centre at **Q 438**97 **098**64.

Hillwalkers along the Brandon ridge, with Brandon Mountain behind.

With the stream now on the right, continue to follow the white posts uphill on a grassy path to another pile of rocks marked by a cross: this is the first Station on the *Cosán na Naomh*. The track passes two other Stations, becomes peaty and stony until reaching a standing stone with a small pile of rock beside a white post near the fourth Station. The track becomes even stonier still after this and the slope steepens and becomes rockier until reaching the next Station. The slope flattens somewhat after this, reaching a standing stone on a rocky mound before reaching the sixth Station. The route progresses onward uphill from here, charting its way along a further eight Stations. It passes an area of rocky outcrops splattered on the grassy slope, winds along the side of a spur, and then meets a wall before the final pull up to the summit of Brandon Mountain.

Once at the summit, retrace steps from there back to the start.

Brandon Ridge Variation

It is possible to continue from Brandon Mountain along the ridge, taking in Brandon Peak and Gearhane along the way as described in the previous route. Continue until reaching the Green Man sign (**Q 468**24 **087**73 in Route 9). From here descend south-west, then swing south along a boggy plateau to arrive at a track at **Q 457**50 **067**50 just before the col. Follow the track, marked on the OSi map as The Pilgrims' Route, as it meanders down the western flanks on the mountain above Glin North until eventually reaching a lane. Continue south-west down this lane until reaching a junction. Turn right at the junction and walk along the minor road, taking a right at the fork at **Q 421**00 **083**50 and then a right again at the signpost for Mt Brandon back to the start point at the cul-de-sac (**Q 433**90 **094**33).

Brandon Mountain via Paternoster Lakes

A challenging approach along one of the finest glacial corries and mountain ridge in Ireland – a true classic!

Grade:	5
Distance:	16km (10 miles)
Ascent:	1,080m (3,543ft)
Time:	6½–7½ hours, time added for difficulty of terrain
Map:	OSi 1:50,000 Sheet 70 or OSi 1:25,000 Brandon Mountain

Start/finish: Turn left along a narrow road known locally as The Pilgrim's Route after the bridge over the Owenmore River and before Cloghane village. Continue for around 3.3km (2 miles) to park at a small lay-by near a bridge where there are spaces for two cars at **Q 490**₉₈ **084**₆₁ (Point A). There are spaces for another 2 cars around 3km (1¾ miles) further at the cul-de-sac at **Q 470**₄₂ **068**₆₁ (Point B), or you may leave a second car there to avoid the road walk at the end.

Brandon Peak rising above Loch Cruite. The waterfall flowing down from Loch Nalacken is at its far end. The route ascends stacked glacial valleys beyond this culminating on Brandon Mountain.

A paternoster lake is one of a series of glacial lakes connected by a single stream. They climb a valley one after another to a corrie which contains a *cirque* (French for 'arena') lake surrounded by an amphitheatre of mountains. The name comes from the Latin word Paternoster, meaning 'Lord's Prayer'. Paternoster lakes are so called as they have a resemblance to rosary beads. The Dingle Peninsula's paternoster lakes are under the precipitous, rocky walls of the Brandon massif. This classic route follows the course of these lakes, a level at a time, until meeting the Faha path at the head of its magnificent glacial corrie. From there, traverse the Brandon ridge as described in Route 9 before descending to The Pilgrim's Route to complete the circuit.

Route Description

From Point A, walk around 600m back along the road to reach a boreen with a 'Loch Cruite Cottage' signpost at **Q 493**₆₀ **089**₈₇. Turn left into the boreen after a house. Reach a green and white painted cottage at a bend after around 150m. Go through a rusted metal gate to the left of the cottage,

Loch Nalacken. The route to the next glacial valley above climbs steeply on the grassy slope to the left of the rocky crag at the waterfall on its far end, before veering right back to the top of the falls.

followed by another metal gate soon after.

Ascend a grassy track for around 400m uphill to reach a fork at **Q 491**₈₅ **092**₇₄. There is a clump of trees to the left and Brandon Peak projects skyward behind. Take the left fork and walk towards the trees. The track dwindles to an indistinct path after a bend. Follow the path and cross the fence at its end at **Q 489**₅₈ **093**₇₃.

Continue uphill on the grassy hillside toward Brandon Peak, which is dominated by a steep rocky spur lined with vertiginous crags. Arrive on a flat, grassy section overlooking Loch Cruite ('Harp Lake') at its south-eastern end. Here, enjoy the grandeur of a natural amphitheatre adorned with waterfalls, streams, crags, cliffs and peaks. Loch Cruite is the first and largest in the string of paternoster lakes, each higher than the other along the glacial corrie to the north-west.

Contour along the grassy hillside just above Loch Cruite on its eastern end. Around the lake's midpoint, veer right and ascend the slope to the top of a spur. The pyramidal rocky wall of Brandon Peak projects skyward across the lake. To its right is the wide scree and field of Garrán Ceoil or 'ugly/grain music', the 'music' probably referring to tumbling rocks or boulders.

Continue north-west along the spur for a few hundred metres to reach a fence at **Q 481**₀₂ **106**₇₃. Cross the fence and follow a grassy path close to it. The terrain here is full of scattered rocks and boulders. Leave the fence to reach the southern end of Loch Nalacken (*Loch na Lacha*, 'Duck Lake'). There is a waterfall on its far side which plunges down a rocky headwall.

Waterfall at Loch Nalacken.

Cross the outflow of Loch Nalacken and follow an intermittent path by the lakeshore to its northern end near the waterfall. Before reaching the waterfall, ascend the grassy steep ground strewn with rocks and boulders – well to the left of the rocky headwall. Although steep, it is easier than it looks as the slope is mainly on short grass. Ascend to a level above the headwall and waterfall, and reach a grassy area at **Q 472**70 **108**51 below some overhanging crags.

Keeping the crags to your left (and the waterfall well away to the right), contour along an indistinct path to reach an area of massive sandstone slabs. The gigantic slabs reduce in size upon reaching a small lake. In fact, this is the beginning of a series of small lakes, all linked with adjoining streams cascading on rocky slabs. The mountain scenery here is quite stupendous, dominated by sheer rocky walls and curved rock layers that guard the eastern flanks of Brandon Mountain.

Follow the lakeshore around the first lake, keeping it to your right. It leads to another small lake beyond. Follow this around to meet a small stream and cross it at **Q 471**06 **111**72. Keep to the right of all subsequent lakes and pick a way up the grassy and rocky terrain. Ascend the narrowing glacial corrie a level at a time to meet the Faha path in the boulder-filled amphitheatre above (**Q 465**04 **118**52 where there is a yellow arrow on rock in Route 9).

Continue beyond this point toward the ridge-top and then along the Brandon ridge to finally descend the zigzags at Fallaghnamara down to the minor road of The Pilgrim's Route. This section of the walk is described in detail in Route 9. Once on the road, simply follow it back to the car at Point A or B.

Loch Nalacken and Loch Cruite, with Brandon Peak to the right.

Ballysitteragh, Beennabrack and An Bhinn Dubh

This moderate, varied circuit goes off the beaten track from the top of the Conor Pass.

Grade:	3
Distance:	11km (6¾ miles)
Ascent:	610m (2,001ft)
Time:	3¾–4¾ hours
Map:	OSi 1:50,000 Sheet 70 or OSi 1:25,000 *Brandon Mountain*

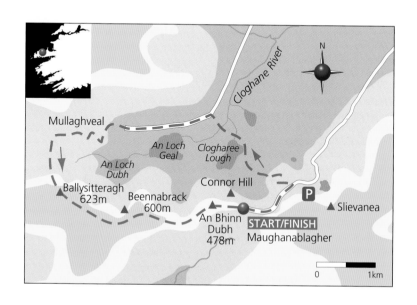

START/FINISH: The highest point on the Conor Pass Road at **Q 490**41 **055**83, where there are spaces for many cars.

Looking down on vales of Cloghane and Owenmore, flanked by Brandon on the left and Slievanea on the right, from the slopes of An Bhinn Dubh.

The Conor Pass road was built as part of Famine-relief efforts. The men involved in its construction were provided with soup. Ironically, they died sooner than they would have without working for those rations as the soup was of poor nutritional value. From the top of the Conor Pass, the route goes down into a wide, lonely valley with ancient field systems, ruined stone dwellings and mysterious lakes. As you walk along blanket bog, russet heather-clad slopes and the summits of Ballysitteragh (623m/2,044ft), Beennabrack (600m/1,968ft) and An Bhinn Dubh (478m/1,568ft), you are always under the shadow of mighty Brandon.

Route Description

Walk down the Conor Pass road away from Dingle town as it winds its way along a narrow section under the Maughanablagher Cliffs. About 1km on, notice a metal gate on the left at **Q 498**22 **059**94. This gate leads to a grassy, stony track that zigzags down the hillside into the Cloghane valley where several lakes sit. After an area littered with small boulders, you will soon arrive at some ruined stone dwellings, surrounded by stone-walled fields at **Q 490**70 **064**10.

This is an area where Blackface sheep roam and ravens soar in the sky. The boulder-strewn slopes are decorated with bracken, sphagnum moss, star moss and compact rush near the shores of Clogharee Lough.

Walk to the north-eastern end of the lake where there is a fence at **Q 490**29 **066**11. Here, staghorn lichen grows amongst the clumps of moor grass and ling heather. Follow the water's edge. About 150m away you will reach another fence: cross it at a low gap at **Q 488**93 **067**43. Later cross a stream to a field lined with moor grass, ling heather and gorse. Continue walking north-westward to reach a bend at another stream. Cross this, and you will arrive at a green track at **Q 485**94 **070**11.

Clogharee Lough, Lough Atlea and An Loch Geal on the Cloghane valley floor with Brandon Peak rising behind, as seen from the Conor Pass road.

There is a metal gate at the end of the track. On the right of the gate, by a section of stone wall, there is a portion of fence with a wooden stile of sorts. You are now on the section of road known as The Pilgrims' Route. Follow the road westward toward Mullaghveal. The tarmac ends after about 1.5km of road, near the farmhouse on the left.

The Pilgrims' Route now becomes a track that leads westward to the obvious col above. Go through six gates, some accompanied by stiles, along the track as it zigzags up the slope. The predominantly grassy track becomes increasingly stony as you walk under some electric posts just before the col.

Next, walk to the corner of some fences at **Q 457**91 **067**25. Cross the fence here and ascend southward on the grassy and mossy slope, keeping the line of fences to your left. Midway up, the spur veers south-eastward. Continue following the fence to the grassy plateau which is adorned with wood rush and staghorn lichen.

As you approach the summit of Ballysitteragh, veer away from the fence to reach a pile of rocks at **Q 460**55 **057**16. For a flat summit, Ballysitteragh offers amazing 360° views of the Dingle Peninsula, and especially that of Dingle town, harbour and bay to the south.

From Ballysitteragh, walk south-eastward toward a broad col. There is a fence corner at **Q 463**71 **055**55. Continue following the fence to the summit of Beennabrack, and then eastward down a col, followed by a slight rise to An Bhinn Dubh ('the black peak') before descending to meet the Conor Pass road again.

In the 1950s, a child's body was found in the peat, completely preserved. She was said to be from the seventh or eighth century. She had red hair, wore a dress and held a purse in her hand.

The striated eastern cliffs of Ballysitteragh.

Slievanea Loop from Conor Pass

This route explores glacial corries above the Conor Pass with fabulous views toward the Brandon massif.

Grade:	3
Distance:	9.5km (6 miles)
Ascent:	540m (1,772ft)
Time:	3¼–4 hours
Map:	OSi 1:50,000 Sheet 70 or OSi 1:25,000 *Brandon Mountain*

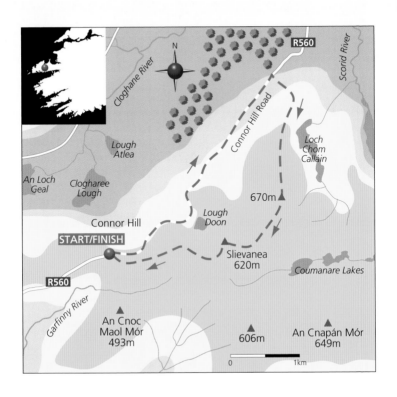

Start/finish: Car park at the top of the Conor Pass road at **Q 490**₄₂ **055**₈₃.

The waterfall that falls from Loch Doon, along the Conor Pass road.

The Swiss naturalist Louis Agassiz proposed in 1837 that Europe had once been enveloped by glaciers and ice sheets. He called his theory *die Eiszeit* or Ice Age and suggested that it would explain features in the landscape such as erratics, corries, drumlins and gravel banks. Agassiz had visited Ireland on several occasions during that time and made note of some features to suggest an Irish Ice Age. But it was not until 1849 that an important breakthrough was made. Alpine mountaineer John Ball visited Lough Doon (also known as Pedlar's Lake) on the Conor Pass and accumulated conclusive evidence that its corrie was similar to ones in Switzerland, where glaciers still exist. This moderate route visits the site where Ball made his discovery before ascending the hillside at Kilmore to the top of a spur overlooking Loch Chom Calláin. The spur leads to the summits of Slievanea Northeast Top (670m/2,198ft) and Slievanea (620m/2,034ft), where the glacial landscape of Lough Doon can be admired in its entirety from above.

Loch Chom Calláin with Slievenalecka (right) and Slievenagower (left) rising behind from the spur above Kilmore.

Looking down on Slievenalecka and Slievenagower from cliffs below the summit of Slievanea northeast top.

Route Description

Walk down the Conor Pass road away from Dingle town, keeping a stone wall on your left. The deep, wide valley runs below where the Cloghane and Owenmore rivers chart their course. A collection of lakes also sit in this glacial valley, which is dominated by the sweeping arc of Brandon Peak towering behind. The road is narrow, with passing places along some sections and overhanging crags hugging its rightmost fringes.

Reach a car park on the right around 1.5km away at **Q 502**₆₇ **061**₁₉. A waterfall gracefully tumbles down a rocky enclave from Lough Doon in the corrie above. The entire scenery toward the corrie is composed of rock: large boulders, striated slabs, vertiginous crags and the contorted cliffs that guard the northern flanks of Slievanea. Striations in the Old Red Sandstone were produced by stones in the ice as it flowed from the corrie above during the Ice Age. A glance across the impressive Owenmore valley reveals Loch Cruite and the stunning backdrop of the Brandon massif.

The stone wall disappears for a time further along the road as the hillside on the right becomes grassier. Just as it reappears, the wall ends abruptly again before a young conifer forest on the left at Kilmore. Just before reaching the end of the wall, a gravel track appears on the right near a concrete building.

There is a metal gate on the right of the track and another further to the left by a fence. Head towards a metal gate to the left at **Q 514**₅₄ **079**₈₈. Ascend the grassy and mossy slope beyond, avoiding patches of tussocky grass and bracken, to reach the spur above. The view eastward is good, with Loch Chom Calláin sitting in the valley below. A waterfall plunges into Loch an Dúin in the next valley, framed by a backdrop of hills including Slievenalecka and Slievenagower. The Scorid River flows from both Loch Chom Calláin and Loch an Dúin into the waters of Brandon Bay to the north.

The area around the Scorid River and Loch an Dúin is a haven for archaeologists and historians alike. A series of Neolithic and Bronze Age markers pre-dating the formation of the blanket bog exist to the west and on a low hillock to the east of the river. There are rock art boulders, drystone huts, pre-bog field systems, a wedge tomb and standing stones all embedded into the landscape.

When ready, veer right and ascend the grassy spur. It is broad initially but later narrows, rising elegantly to Slievanea Northeast Top (summit 670m on the map) above. A line of crags can be seen to the left, running across the steep ground above Loch Chom Calláin. After a heathery patch, the terrain turns rocky and steepens near the top. Continue until reaching the broad, grassy top and arrive at a pile of rocks at **Q 515**80 **063**65 marking the summit.

Descend south-westward from the summit on a gentle, grassy slope to reach an area of peat hags. Veer right and westward as soon as a narrow lake-filled corrie below comes into view. Continue along the clifftop and soon a second corrie, housing Loch Doon, appears at the base of precipitous cliffs below.

Pick up a sheep path near the clifftop to reach the unmarked grassy top of Slievanea (*Sliabh Mhacha Ré*, 'mountain of the smooth plain') at **Q 507**45 **057**51. Veer northward for a few metres to gain this top, taking care not to step too close to the cliff edge. It is easy to see how the mountain got its name from the wide expanse of moorland to the south and south-west. Views down to Loch Doon and its cliff-rimmed glacial corrie are impressive, with the Brandon massif behind.

From Slievanea, follow the sheep path along the clifftop to reach a stone enclosure at **Q 502**56 **056**25. Keep to the left of a fence near the clifftop and descend westward down a gentle slope. At the end of the fence, veer right and descend a grassy slope. Follow an intermittent path to reach a broad stony track above the Conor Pass road. Cross the road back to the car park at the start.

Looking across to cliffs and down to Loch Doon and the Conor Pass Road from Slievanea.

Ballyduff to Anascaul

Take a scenic walk along central Dingle's finest valley and cross a barren mountain plateau to drop into the legendary valley of Anascaul.

Grade:	2
Distance:	13.5km (8½ miles)
Ascent:	300m (984ft)
Time:	4–5 hours
Map:	OSi 1:50,000 Sheet 70 or OSi 1:25,000 *Brandon Mountain*

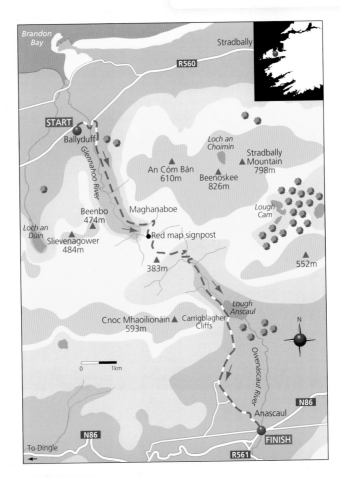

Start: Parking spaces at Ballyduff graveyard at **Q 540**₇₀ **101**₀₀, just off the R560, due east of Cloghane village.
Finish: South Pole Inn, Anascaul Village.

This route, over a mountain plateau to Anascaul, begins at Ballyduff (An Baile Dubh, 'black village') graveyard. The area is associated with the Celtic deity Crom Dubh, a god of fertility and harvest. According to local tales, a tailor by the name of Sean Conway once lived nearby. One night Conway spotted a funeral cortège going up the road to Ballyduff graveyard. However, the next

The Glennahoo River can be seen twisting along its partially shadowed valley floor with Beenbo rising behind.

day he learnt that not a soul in Ballyduff was dead so it was believed that the cortège was a fairy funeral. From Ballyduff, the route follows a fine track along the long and scenic Glennahoo valley toward Maghanaboe (*Macha na Bó*, 'milking field of the cow'). The sense of remoteness is heightened as the track contours up the hillside to reach the top of a barren and expansive plateau below Beenoskee. A crossing of the plateau is assisted by a mountain path which descends into the dramatic, cliff-rimmed Anascaul valley on the opposite end. Walk in the footsteps of the Antarctic explorer Tom Crean by following an old road beyond the lake toward the quiet village of Anascaul (*Átha na Scáil*, 'river of the hero'), named after its associations with the legendary Cú Chulainn.

Route Description

Walk back towards the R560 from the graveyard and turn right. Walk around 500m along the road and cross the bridge over the Glennahoo River. Take care while walking along the R560 as it is a busy road with no verges.

After crossing the bridge, continue along the R560 for another 300m. Leave the R560 and turn right into a track at **Q 546**₀₀**103**₅₀. There is a small converted farmhouse with dormer windows and a sloped flat roof extension at the track entrance. The track is bordered by stone walls overgrown with fern, gorse and moss. Follow the track uphill. Ignore a narrow, informal grassy path on the left and continue to pass a large farmhouse, also on the left.

Lough Anascaul and cliffs of Reamore to its right. The footpath to the left of the lake descends from the hillside at its far end.

Pass a lane on the right. Ignore it and continue ahead (southwards) to Maghanaboe at the head of the valley. The Glennahoo River twists and turns along the valley floor to the right. The narrow valley, some 3km long, is flanked by a sweep of steep slopes clothed with banks of scree.

Arrive above some ruined stone cottages surrounded by stone walls near the end of the valley at Maghanaboe (**Q 556**34 **075**30), where herds of cattle once grazed the plains. In the nineteenth century, the Dineen and O'Donnell families eked out a living here.

Here, the track veers left and climbs uphill above a narrow stream-filled ravine to the right. The stream ripples with cascades and is decorated with rock shelves of various shapes and sizes. Fringed by holly trees and fraughan, the delightful track is also graced with pockets of common violets, tormentils and primroses. Clumps of St Patrick's cabbage, part of the Lusitanian flora, hide in the damp rock crevices with its star-shaped pink-white flowers adding further colour in the summer.

The track contours the hillside and leads to a notch at a bend above the ravine. It crosses the stream at **Q 562**50 **076**41. This is a wonderfully scenic spot. Several large, grassy hillocks are visible to the north-east where several streams tumble down rock faults.

The track veers right after crossing the stream and ascends gradually south-west uphill, with the ravine now below to the right. The track soon dwindles to a path to reach a Red Man signpost at **Q 560**45 **072**07 overlooking the top of Maghanaboe.* (This reference point is used in the next walk.)

After crossing a stream, the path contours across the hillside before rising gradually to the top of a moorland plateau. There is a Red Man marker post at **Q 564**₂₂ **067**₄₉ just below point 383m on the plateau.

Head eastward for just over 100m to arrive at a pile of rocks at **Q 565**₆₂ **067**₂₉. Continue ahead to reach a cairn around another 100m away. The path is now stony and rocky, but later becomes a grassy and boggy track, and zigzags downhill. Some delightful cascades tumble to your right. The track crosses three stone bridges. At the third bridge, two streams spill from the grassy and rocky slopes above, converge, and flow down the beautiful Anascaul valley.

The valley is flanked by fractured cliffs on either side and idyllic Loch Anscaul is soon visible. The track becomes drier and is filled with stones and rocks, and then grass, before reaching a metal gate with a ladder stile at **Q 574**₄₁ **062**₄₅. In the summer, fragrant chamomile grows along the sides.

The track passes another two metal gates and runs close to a stream on the left. The valley is flanked by cliffs riven with gullies: An Ré Mhór on the left and An Com Dubh on the right. The track meanders on until Loch Anscaul is close on the left and then soon reaches a car park by the lake below the Carrigblagher cliffs.

The track becomes a potholed tarmac lane flanked by a stone wall and gorse bushes. The lane gradually rises to a metal gate at **Q 583**₅₉ **045**₆₉. Follow the narrow tarmac lane as it winds its way past some fields and houses for about 1.5km to reach a crossroad at **Q 580**₁₂ **031**₈₁. There are signs for Ballynacourty Cemetery and Tom Crean's grave straight ahead. Ignore those but instead take a left at the crossroad.

Continue along the straight byroad for just under 1km, to reach a farmhouse on the right. The road weaves its way for about another 1km to reach a T-junction. Turn left here on to the N86 and cross a bridge over the Anascaul River. Arrive at the legendary South Pole Inn (on the left immediately after the bridge) and enter for a celebratory pint of Tom Crean's lager! (For an account of Tom Crean's life, read Michael Smith's *An Unsung Hero*).

Tom Crean's South Pole Inn at Anascaul village.

Beenbo, Slievenagower, Slievenalecka and An Cnapán Mór

This varied route explores dramatic corries, hidden mountain lakes and many summits above the Maghanaboe in Central Dingle.

Grade:	4
Distance:	22km (13¾ miles)
Ascent:	900m (2,953ft)
Time:	7–8¾ hours
Map:	OSi 1:50,000 Sheet 70 or OSi 1:25,000 *Brandon Mountain*

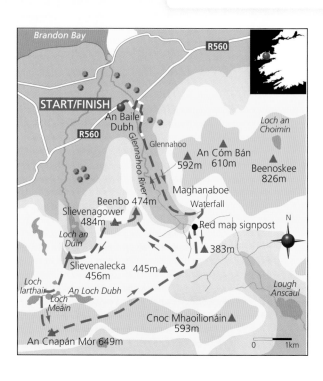

Start/Finish: Parking spaces at Ballyduff or An Baile Dubh graveyard at **Q 540**₇₀ **101**₀₀, just off the R560, due east of the village of Cloghane.

The view from Slievenagower across Loch an Dúin to Slievenalecka and Slievenea North-east Top.

The townland of Ballyduff (*An Baile Dubh*, 'black village') is associated with the Celtic deity Crom Dubh, a god of fertility and harvest. A harvest ritual, known as Domhnach Crom Dubh, was celebrated by the Iron Age Celts. Starting from Ballyduff graveyard, this route approaches the beak-shaped hill of Beenbo (474m/1,555ft) by way of Maghanaboe – a long, remote valley that follows the twisting course of the Glennahoo River. Following the edge of a barren mountain plateau, we continue over the summits of Slievenagower (484m/1,588ft) and Slievenalecka (456m/1,496ft), which give dramatic views down into lake-filled corries. Some remote mountain lakes surrounded by sheer rocky walls are visited after, deep in the heart of the plateau. With the summit of An Cnapán Mór (649m/2,129ft) as the icing on the cake, the plateau is again negotiated before returning via Maghanaboe. As the plateau can be difficult to navigate in the mist, clear weather is recommended for this route.

Route Description

The initial part of this walk from Ballyduff graveyard and along Maghanaboe is described up to the Red Man signpost (*) at **Q 560**₄₅ **072**₀₇ in the previous route.

Cross the stream here and head southwards to meet a black post at **Q 561**₇₇ **069**₆₇. Contour below the western slopes of point 383m, keeping a stream away to your right. Reach a flat area after around 750m, then veer right (north-west) by contouring the hillside at the base of summit 445m. The terrain undulates slightly and after around 1km cross a stream.

Ascend the hillside beyond the stream, still in a north-westerly direction, for another 1km to reach the summit of Beenbo.

The grassy and mossy summit of Beenbo at **Q 545**39 **074**59 is unmarked. The Irish name on the OSi map is Gob an Iolair ('beak of the eagle'), which does not match up with the anglicised version. Beenbo sounds more like Binn Bó or 'peak of the cattle', which seems to relate to the other place names of the area: for instance, Maghanaboe or *Macha na Bó* in the valley below means 'milking field of the cow'. However, when viewed from the sky, Beenbo does resemble an eagle's beak.

Views from the summit are good and include the Brandon range to the west and the beak-shaped hills of Slievenagower and Slievenalecka to the south-west. Glennahoo spreads out to the east, with the track rising up the hillside from Maghanaboe clearly visible, and Beenoskee towering behind. There are also fine views northward down the crest of the ridge toward Ballyduff, with Brandon Bay as the backdrop.

Descend south-westward from Beenbo and cross a fence at the col to rise again to the summit of Slievenagower, the 'mountain of the goat'. There is no cairn at its highest point at **Q 539**60 **072**26.

Carry on westward from the summit for some 250m to the edge of a steep heather-clad slope at **Q 536**71 **071**40 to be greeted by one of the finest views on the entire peninsula. The blue lake of Loch an Dúin stretches out for nearly 1km below, with a green island just off its centre. Slievenalecka and Slievanea's Northeast Top project sharply skyward beyond the lake, and the entire Brandon ridge sweeps the skyline in the distance. You may find it hard to leave.

Next, descend south-westward down rugged slopes, aiming for a col. There is a stone shelter near the col, and a waterfall plunging down the valley below also comes into sight. Cross a stream at the rugged gap at **Q 534**11 **065**32 and ascend the slopes ahead, keeping a line of fences to your right, to the summit of Slievenalecka (*An Starraicín*, 'the steeple') at **Q 527**77 **064**11.

Descend south-westward from Slievenalecka on rough moorland and an area of peat hags for about a distance of 800m to Loch Meáin, one of the Coumanare lakes. Walk along the rocky northern end of Loch Meáin to a waterway that connects it to Loch Iarthair. A good spot to stop for lunch is at **Q 520**17 **055**38 just above the waters of Loch Iarthair. Silence and solitude abound. The lakes sit in a remote hollow flanked by fearsome cliffs to the south and steep slopes to the west.

Our objective is a prominent spur between the two lakes, due south. Cross the waterway and ascend the rocky spur, weaving around rock slabs and along grassy ledges. The landscape below is impressive: the long arm of Slievanea towers above Loch Iarthair, and all the hills you walked on previously, including Beenoskee beyond, can be seen to the north-east. The best views are at **Q 520**17 **052**41, just before the slope starts to get steep.

Ascend the steep, grassy slope until its gradient eases near the top of the plateau. Aim for the obvious highest point ahead, due south-east. It gets stony near the summit of the big lump of An Cnapán Mór, where a trig point and a cairn greet you at **Q 522**$_{26}$ **045**$_{90}$. Views to the south of Dingle Bay across to the Iveragh Peninsula are good.

From the summit, descend eastward on moderate, stony slopes that later becomes grassy. Meet a stony track about 1.5km away at **Q 536**$_{96}$ **050**$_{13}$, just north of the col at Windy Gap. Follow this track for another 1.3km until it peters out around a broad gap at **Q 548**$_{93}$ **057**$_{10}$.

Here, keep the high ground to your left and contour under it, aiming for the lower ground south-west of summit 383m just over 1km away. There are traces of a faint path at times, but it is mainly trackless, grassy and stony terrain. The rough ground drops steadily around **Q 556**$_{78}$ **058**$_{78}$, and here aim north-eastward for a distance of 500m to reach a flat grassy area.

At **Q 560**$_{17}$ **062**$_{43}$, it starts to rise again. There is a group of rocks scattered amongst an area of tussocky grass, compact rush and heather. Keep higher ground to your right and contour underneath. When you are just under summit 383m, veer northward to meet some black posts at **Q 561**$_{77}$ **069**$_{67}$.

Follow the path to a Red Man sign-post at **Q 560**$_{45}$ **072**$_{07}$ overlooking the top of Maghanaboe. From there, retrace steps down into Maghanaboe and along the Glennahoo valley back to the start at Ballyduff.

Descending into the Maghanaboe valley.

Cnoc Mhaolionáin and An Bhánog Thuaidh

Walk in the footsteps of legends over the scenic hills of Loch Anscaul.

Grade:	3
Distance:	10km (6¼ miles)
Ascent:	650m (2,133ft)
Time:	3½–4½ hours
Map:	OSi 1:50,000 Sheet 70 or OSi 1:25,000 *Brandon Mountain*

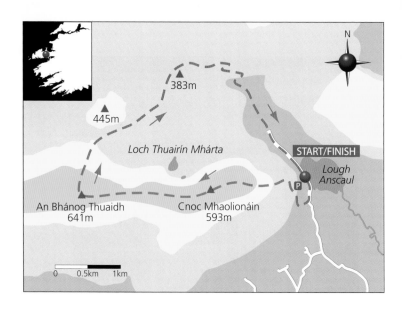

Start/Finish: Just beyond the South Pole Inn at Anascaul village, turn right after a bridge onto a minor road signposted 'Anascaul Lake'. Follow this and take a right upon reaching a crossroad. Drive to its end, pass through gates and park by spaces near Loch Anscaul at **Q 582**₄₈ **051**₀₉ – just below the rock-strewn slopes, precipitous cliffs and gullies of Carrigblagher.

In Anascaul there is a pub named the South Pole Inn. Its owner was a local man, Tom Crean, who was second officer to Ernest Shackleton, the great Antarctic explorer. Crean enlisted with the Royal Navy just before his 16th birthday and played a heroic role in the ill-fated 1911–13 Scott expedition to the South Pole. He was also part of Shackleton's 1914–16 *Endurance* expedition. This walk explores the hills of

Looking northeastwards from near the top of the Carrigblagher Cliffs towards the back of the Anascaul valley, with Beenoskee towering behind.

Crean's backyard, in a picturesque valley flanked by steep cliffs around Loch Anscaul. It is one of my favourite areas in the Dingle Peninsula, with the valley and mountains itself wreathed in legends. Two summits are visited in this walk: Cnoc Mhaoilionáin (593m/1,946ft) and An Bhánóg Thuaidh (641m/2,103ft).

Route Description

Walk back a distance of just over 400m south along the road to **Q 582**₉₈ **047**₁₇. A fence zigzags up the green slopes on your right, beside a stream. Keep the fence and stream to your left and ascend south-westward up the gradual, grassy slope. There are traces of a faint path leading to a clump of gorse about a distance of 150m up the hill at **Q 581**₇₆ **046**₉₃.

Here veer north-westward, zigzagging up the moderately steep slopes and follow the line of the Carrigblagher Cliffs (while keeping a safe distance from the edge). The grassy and rocky slope, although sustained, is always manageable, and at times there is evidence of a trodden path. The valley below starts to open up as you ascend, but the best view overall is at the eastern end of the spur at **Q 579**₄₈ **050**₇₂.

The entire valley at the back of Loch Anscaul, with the Garrivagh River twisting and turning, can be appreciated. Beenoskee (826m/2,710ft) towers above the sharp cliffs of Reamore to the north. Loch Anscaul itself appears like a dark-blue carpet far below, resting by the fertile slopes of Dromavally.

Lough Anscaul, Reamore and Dromavally as seen from the Cnoc Mhaoilionáin spur.

Loch Anscaul is named after Scál Ní Mhurnáin, one of Cú Chulainn's many women. She was taken captive by a giant and held at the lake. Cú Chulainn charged up the high ground of Reamore and hurled fiery boulders at the giant, who stood where you stand now. Cú Chulainn suddenly gave a loud groan and Scál, believing her lover had been killed, drowned herself in the lake.

On flat high ground north-east of Reamore is a large pile of standing stones with a collapsed inner chamber, said to be Cú Chulainn's House. However, it pre-dates the legendary hero by a thousand years so it is more likely a Bronze Age burial mound for noble tribesmen.

Next, ascend the straightforward spur leading west toward Cnoc Mhaoilionáin. There is a cairn at the top of the spur at **Q 572**69 **050**47, and from here undulating terrain leads you to the twin cairns on the summit of Cnoc Mhaoilionáin at **Q 568**15 **048**84. The mountains of the Dingle Peninsula will fill your view to the west, north and east on the summit. Across the waters of Dingle Bay the peaks of the MacGillycuddy's Reeks can also seen on a clear day.

From here, simply follow the broad ridge west. The terrain is of mixed grass and peat and there is a good trodden path. It is a pleasant stroll on the undulating ridge with wonderful all-round views. A line of posts follows the ridge line, and later you will cross some fences to arrive at a peaty area above two lakes, with the range of hills from Glennahoo to Stradbally Mountain prominent in the background. A broad col then leads to slopes which rise to a mossy and stony summit area, culminating with a small pile of rocks at **Q 548**30 **048**27 marking the top of An Bhánóg Thuaidh.

The panoramic view from Cnoc Mhaoilionáin's slopes includes all the hills of central Dingle and the Brandon range to the northwest.

Loch Thuairín Mhárta and the peaks ranging from Glennahoo to Stradbally Mountain in the distance.

The view across the Owenmore valley toward the sharp eastern side of Brandon, with Loch Cruite and the paternoster route is particularly impressive.

From the summit of An Bhánóg Thuaidh head northward, then veer north-eastward to descend a steep slope of grass and heather, adorned with staghorn lichen. Aim for a broad grassy area south of summit 445m that can be quite boggy on wet days. However, there is a stony patch at **Q 550**48 **055**30 for a rest if required.

Here, keep the high ground to your left and contour under it, aiming for the lower ground south-west of summit 383m just over 1km away. There are traces of a faint path at times, but it is mainly trackless grassy and stony terrain. The rough ground drops steadily around **Q 556**78 **058**78, and here aim north-eastward for a distance of 500m to reach a flat, grassy area.

At **Q 560**17 **062**43, it starts to rise again. Rocks are scattered amongst an area of tussocky grass, compact rush and heather. Keep higher ground to your right and contour along trackless terrain underneath. When you are just under summit 383m, go up a slight rise leading to the north-east of it and arrive at a Red Man marker post at **Q 564**22 **067**49.

Go east for a distance of just over 100m to arrive at a pile of rocks at **Q 565**62 **067**29. Continue on straight ahead on the track to reach a cairn about a 100m away. The track becomes stony and rocky initially, then later grassy and boggy, as it zigzags down the mountainside.

Views down the Anascaul valley are lovely as you descend, and some delightful cascades tumble to your right. You will cross three stone bridges. At the third bridge, two streams spill from the grassy and rocky slopes above and converge.

The track becomes drier after this and the valley is flanked by fractured cliffs on either side as you descend. The track is initially rocky, but later grassy, as you reach a metal gate with a ladder stile at **Q 574**41 **062**45. In the height of summer, chamomile can be seen growing along the sides.

Go through two metal gates, as the stream twists and turns on your left below the cliffs of Reamore.

Follow the track, with the waters of Loch Anscaul now on your left, back to the car park by the lake.

79

ROUTE 17:

Stradbally Mountain, Beenoskee, An Com Bán And Binn An Tuair

A strenuous route over four peaks of northern Anascaul.

Grade:	4
Distance:	15km (9¼ miles)
Ascent:	910m (2,986ft)
Time:	5¼–6½ hours
Map:	OSi 1:50,000 Sheet 70 or OSi 1:25,000 *Brandon Mountain*

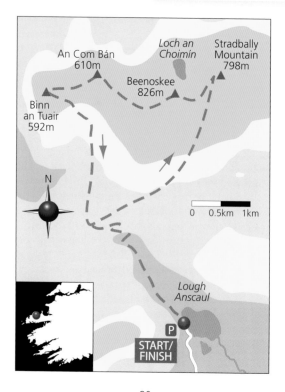

Start/Finish: At the parking space near Loch Anscaul at **Q 582**₄₈ **051**₀₉ as in Route 16.

Looking southeastwards down the Anascaul Valley, flanked by the cliffs of Reamore (left) and Carrigblagher (right).

We revisit Anascaul valley and lake in this walk. The first hour or so is exactly the descent route of Route 16, but in reverse. Once on the broad plateau, however, we strike across trackless ground to Stradbally Mountain (798m/2,618ft), and from there walk across a line of peaks consisting of Beenoskee (826m/2,710ft), An Com Bán (610m/2,001ft) and Binn an Tuair (592m/1,942ft). These are the four summits north of Anascaul that provide a bird's-eye view of much of the Dingle Peninsula.

Route Description

Ascend the Anascaul valley on the track, passing two gates with the stream on your right and cliffs on both sides. Cross three stone bridges, and zigzag up the track by lovely cascades. This is essentially the descent route of Route 16.

As you walk up the track, imagine a remote lake in the upper reaches of the valley. No lake exists today, but local tales suggest there was once one here somewhere below the 'black cliffs' of An Com Dubh. The lake seemingly had a sunken round tower and giant eels inhabiting its waters.

Just before the col between point 396m and summit 383m, you will arrive at a cairn at **Q 566**₆₃ **066**₈₁. It is worth making a mental note of this spot, as you will pass it on the return journey.

At this point, the mountains you are aiming for rise above to the north. Stradbally Mountain is at its rightmost end, and this is your first port of call. Set a course north-eastward across the open mountainside on trackless ground to its summit. The terrain consists of moorland at first but later becomes stony and rocky, and the slopes get steeper as you approach the summit cairn of Stradbally Mountain at **Q587**₃₅ **091**₄₇. Loch an Choimín sits in a dark hollow west of Stradbally Mountain, below the sharp eastern edge of Beenoskee.

From the summit, descend the rocky terrain to an equally stony col above Loch an Choimín. Then ascend the grassy and stony slope up to the

The view westwards from Stradbally Mountain, with Loch an Choimín below and Brandon Bay and its mountains beyond.

summit cairn of Beenoskee, the 'mountain above the wind', at **Q580**₆₂**088**₈₀.

Views of most of the mountains of Dingle and of Iveragh can be appreciated from Beenoskee's summit. To the north, the curved arc of Brandon Bay is prominent.

A steep slope of stones and some grassy patches leads westward, and then north-westward, from Beenoskee. You eventually arrive at a broad gap of stones and peat hags. From here, continue north-westward up a grassy slope to a fence near the summit of An Com Bán, 'the white hollow'. Cross a fence carefully to reach the summit at **Q567**₇₁ **091**₉₂.

Next, descend south-westward down a grassy slope and some peat hags to a col. A short rise brings you onto the cairnless summit of Binn an Tuair, the 'bleached green hill', at **Q 558**₅₀ **089**₁₃.

The entire jagged eastern end of the Brandon range across the Glennahoo and Owenmore valleys can be fully appreciated from here. The view south-west is impressive too: a tooth-shaped line of brown hills arranged one after the other float across the Maghanaboe valley.

Descend south-eastward from the summit. The rough slope is riddled with peat hags and later becomes covered with more windswept grass. About a kilometre downhill, you will meet a stream in a slight dip at **Q 566**₀₈**084**₀₄. Cross the stream and descend southward on grassy and boggy ground for about 1.6km to reach the cairn at **Q 566**₆₃ **066**₈₁.

Retrace your steps from here to the car park by Loch Anscaul.

Looking across the Glennahoo valley to the Brandon range beyond from the summit slopes of Binn an Tuair.

Magharees Loop

Walk along some of the finest, sandy beaches on the Dingle Peninsula embraced with stunning mountain views.

Normal Variation		Short Variation	
Grade:	1/2	Grade:	1
Distance:	20.5km (12¾ miles)	Distance:	13.5km (8½ miles)
Ascent:	Negligible	Ascent:	Negligible
Time:	5½–6½ hours	Time:	3½–4½ hours
Map:	OSi 1:50,000 Sheet 70, 71	Map:	OSi 1:50,000 Sheet 70, 71

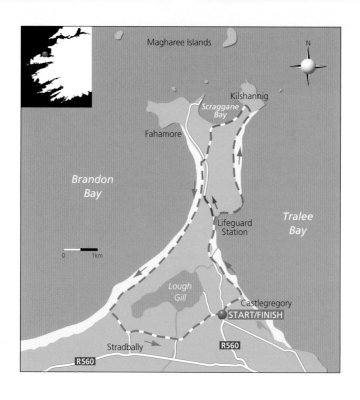

Start/finish: Park at **Q 621**₇₄ **133**₆₂ at the large car park near the Spar shop in Castlegregory village.

Magharees (Na Machairí, 'the plains') is a 5km/3-mile-long peninsula north of Lough Gill and Castlegregory on the Dingle Peninsula. Long, sandy beaches are found on both sides of the peninsula, which separates Brandon Bay on the west from Tralee Bay to the east. The peninsula also provides shelter to Fenit Harbour further east, protecting its waters from large Atlantic swells. Marram grass and sand dunes give way to stony and rocky ground towards Scraggane Bay on the northern tip of the peninsula. To the north of Scraggane Bay lie the rugged Magharee Islands or The Seven Hogs. On the largest, Illauntannig, are the remains of a seventh-century monastic settlement. There are also some Early

Christian remains, such as the Chi Rho Cross, in Kilshannig in the north-east of the peninsula. Starting and ending in the colourful village of Castlegregory, this long-distance route covers the sweeping beaches on both sides of the peninsula, as well as Scraggane Bay. A shorter variation is provided, missing out on the beaches at the upper end of the peninsula.

Castlegregory beach, with the Slieve Mish mountains in the distance.

Route Description

From the large car park, and with the Spar shop on your left, turn right along the road. Pass a school on the right and continue a short distance to reach a crossroad with Moe's Cafe at the corner. Turn right here and pass a school and a GAA pitch to reach a car park at the beach. The beach stretches for several kilometres from Tullaree East to Magherabeg North. Views of Fenit are good across Tralee Bay, with the Slieve Mish Mountains dominating the landscape to the south-east.

Turn left and walk along the beach, with Tralee Bay to the right. Continue for around 1.4km to reach the outflow from Lough Gill, called 'The Trench', to the sea. Turn left here at **Q 618**₂₀ **149**₅₂ and follow a sandy path between long tussocks to reach a bridge by a road.

Veer right and cross the bridge on the road. The Dingle Way, signposted by Yellow Man signs, runs along the narrow road which can be busy with

Surfers at Scraggane Bay, with Brandon Mountain in cloud to the left beyond.

traffic in the summer. After passing two mobile home parks, reach a lifeguard station on the right by a beach.

Turn right here at **Q 617**₇₂ **160**₆₃ toward the beach and follow Yellow Man signposts along a narrow strip of sandy shoreline. The strand becomes pebbly and rocky at a bend.

Short variation: Instead of veering right toward the strand at the lifeguard station, continue along the road for around 800m. Then leave the road and drop onto the beach at Brandon Bay. Turn left and continue as per the Normal Route from there.

Slightly further, the Yellow Man points toward a sandy path fringed with tussocks, away from the beach. The path soon turns grassy and crosses a field, at the end of which a sandy stretch runs alongside a fence. Reach a stone wall when the fence ends and veer right toward the beach again at **Q 623**₄₅ **173**₉₅. This section of beach is normally quieter than the one at Magherabeg.

Walk along the sand for around 1.2km to where it begins to narrow. Look out for a Yellow Man marker at **Q 623**₆₂ **185**₅₉ near a fenced field to the left. Continue ahead across a grassy, unfenced field to reach a stone wall around 700m away at **Q 628**₀₆ **192**₁₉. There is a white bungalow ahead beyond the wall. Veer left and leave The Dingle Way here. Follow a tarmac footpath, passing some houses on the right and a large green lawn on the left to meet a road.

Ignore the Yellow Man signs on the road. Cross the road and drop into Scraggane Bay. Turn left and walk along the beach. The bay is a popular spot for rowers, surfers and windsurfers, and boats can be seen at a pier ahead. *Naomhóg* racing is also popular here and takes place every Sunday during the high season. The *naomhóg* is an Irish boat with a wooden frame over which canvas is stretched. Veer left near the end of the beach and clamber over some boulders to meet the road above.

Walking southwest on the sands at Brandon Bay.

Turn right and follow the road beyond a bend. Pass houses and fields with livestock along the road. Reach a T-junction with a grotto after passing a surfing school on the left. Cross the road at the T-junction and go through a gap in the concrete wall to the left of the grotto. Follow a path beyond the wall to reach the beach at Brandon Bay. Veer left and walk along the beach with the bay to your right.

This beautiful, sandy beach runs for some 12km (7½ miles) in a wide semicircle from Fahamore in the north to Ceann Duimhche in the west. The bay is exposed to the Atlantic and often receives long rolling swells, which can provide excellent surf. The view ahead is swallowed by mountains to the west and south, with Masatiompan, Brandon Mountain, Beenoskee and Stradbally Mountain featuring prominently. The beach is bordered on the left by high sand dunes covered in windswept marram grass.

After some 5.5km along the beach, veer left at a gap through the grass-covered sand dunes at **Q 586**66 **134**45. Follow a sandy path to reach a tarmac road. Continue straight ahead at a junction signposted 'Golf Club' on the left. Pass a burial ground on the right and continue to reach a concrete bridge. Take a left at the fork just after the bridge and follow the road to pass a farmhouse before reaching some buildings at a junction.

Take a left at the junction and continue along the road, passing a church on the right. After just over 1km, pass a narrow lane on the left signposted 'Lough Gill'. Ignore this and continue straight ahead to pass Ned Natterjack's Restaurant and Bar.

The restaurant's name is fitting as the sand dunes and pools of the Magharees create a unique ecosystem for the rare Natterjack toad. Lough Gill is a major breeding ground for the toads from mid spring to early summer. The toads have a poisonous secretion to ward off predators and fill the air with brassy croaking.

Reach a junction after Ned Natterjack's and take a left along Strand Street. You soon arrive back at the crossroad with Moe's Cafe at the corner. Turn right here and walk back to the start.

Glanteenassig Forest and Lakes

An easy, low-level walk in the 'valley of the waterfalls' that will suit all abilities.

Grade:	1
Distance:	10.5km (6½ miles)
Ascent:	150m (492ft)
Time:	3–3¾ hours
Map:	OSi 1:50,000 Sheet 70, 71

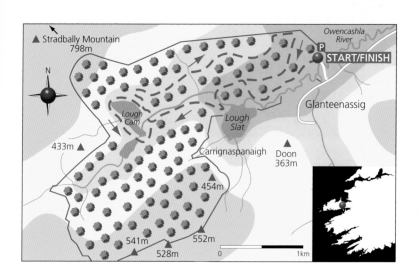

Start/finish: From Tralee, follow the R560 towards Castlegregory. Soon after passing the Seven Hogs Restaurant, look out for a signpost for Glanteenassig Woods on the right-hand side of the road. Leave the R560 there and turn left into a narrow road. Continue for around 4km (2½ miles) passing some houses, farmhouses and wide grassy plains. Turn right near the end of the road to enter a Coillte Forest Recreation Area. There are spaces at a large car park at **Q 620**₂₂ **085**₁₆ after the concrete bridge across the Owencashla River. A noticeboard lists the opening and closing hours of the forest park. If need be, leave a second car at the large car park by Lough Cam at **Q 599**₇₃ **078**₂₀ or at the Glanteenassig Moraine Viewpoint at **Q 600**₀₄ **081**₇₃.

The Owencashla River from near the start of the walk, with the pointed top of Doon rising behind.

Glanteenassig or *Gleann Tí an Easaigh* means 'valley of the waterfalls' and covers more than 450 hectares of mountain, woodland, bog and lake around a sheltered valley. On wet days, several waterfalls tumble down steep cliffs into Lough Slat and Loch Cam, two of the largest lakes in the valley. The underlying geology of the area is Old Red Sandstone, the oldest Devonian rocks in Ireland. A gaze up the cliffs above the lakes reveals the contorted rock strata deposited over the millennia. This is an easy, low-level walk around the foothills and lakes of Glanteenassig. It is suitable for beginners and families with young children as it is entirely on good forest tracks and a boardwalk.

Lough Slat and the cliffs of Carrignaspaniagh to the right.

Route Description

Turn left on the main forest road from the car park. Go through the barriers and walk along the broad vehicle track flanked by trees for around 1.2km to reach a T-junction. Take a left here following the signpost for 'Lakes'. Continue on the track and cross a bridge to reach a car park at a bend at **Q 608**₃₁ **080**₂₃.

Leave the track here and follow a forest path on the left through the woodlands. The woodlands, planted in the 1950s and 1960s, are mainly Sitka spruce and Lodgepole pine. However, there are also pockets of alder, beech, birch, holly, larch and silver fir growing elsewhere in the valley.

The path culminates a short distance away on the edge of Lough Slat. There is a picnic table by some rocks at a sandy section of the reed-filled lake. The lake, gouged out by glaciers during the Ice Age, is surrounded by the sheer cliffs of Carrignaspaniagh ('the Spaniards' rock') on its western end and some smaller crags to the south. A stream tumbles down the green hillside into the lake between the cliffs and crags.

Retrace steps back to the main forest track, turn left and follow it steadily uphill to reach a large car park on the left (signposted 'Viewpoint') overlooking two lakes at **Q 599**₇₃ **078**₂₀. There is a boardwalk around the larger lake, Lough Cam. Cliffs lined with green vegetation and large banks of scree form the corrie headwalls of Lough Cam.

Lough Cam is known for its native brown trout and adult rainbow trout. There are also communities of submerged and floating aquatic species such as the water lily, shoreweed and quillwort.

Follow the boardwalk around the lake in an anticlockwise direction, stopping to read the information boards along the way or to use the picnic tables. On the southern end of the boardwalk, the smaller lake of

Looking at the cliff-lined slopes at the western end of Loch Cam.

An Dúloch comes into view. The boardwalk loops back to the car park at the start.

Retrace steps from the Lough Cam car park back to the main forest track. Take a left and follow the track gradually uphill to reach another car park and picnic tables at the Glanteenassig Moraine Viewpoint at **Q 600**04 **081**73. It is named as such as the forest trail is constructed on a moraine, where a glacial deposit of sand and rock was dumped by a sheet of ice that carved out the valley millennia ago. There are fine views from here toward the forested valley and Lough Slat below. A backdrop of hills including Doon and Cummeen, and the cliffs at Foilnagrave and Carrignaspaniagh complete the panorama.

From the Moraine Viewpoint, continue north-eastward along the track. This is a pleasant stretch with the valley, lake, hills and the Owencashla River winding its way to Tralee Bay on the right and ahead. The hillock of Carrigadav, shaped like a camel's hump, can also be seen to the left. The track meanders downhill to reach a junction.

Turn right at the junction and continue downhill to reach another junction. A left there along the forest track leads back to the start.

ROUTE 20:
Stradbally to Beenoskee from Fermoyle Strand

This challenging circuit from the beach at Fermoyle takes in two peaks of central Dingle, offering commanding views of both land and sea.

Grade:	4
Distance:	25km (15½ miles)
Ascent:	870m (2,854ft)
Time:	8–10 hours
Map:	OSi 1:50,000 Sheet 70/71

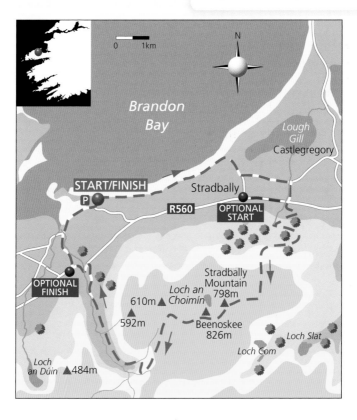

Start/finish: From Tralee, follow the R560 towards Stradbally and Cloghane (*An Clochán*). Leave the R560 around 3.5km (2¼ miles) after Stradbally, veering right onto a minor road leading to Fermoyle Strand and park at **Q 548**₉₃ **122**₄₄. With two cars, you can reduce the walk by 7–8km (2–3 hours) by starting at Tomasin's Bar & Restaurant at Stradbally (**Q 591**₈₅ **122**₂₈) or at the roadside viewpoint around 800m farther away, both with limited parking places. A second car can be left at An Baile Dubh graveyard at **Q 540**₇₀ **101**₀₀ just after the sharp bend over the Glennahoo River.

Fermoyle Strand (Trá Fhormaoileach) is a long, sandy beach sweeping along the foothills of Stradbally Mountain (798m/2,618ft) and its twin peak Beenoskee (826m/2,710ft). The R560 runs south of the beach, passing the rural village of Stradbally. The beach at Fermoyle can be busy on a sunny summer's day and is popular for surfing, bathing and bass fishing. This route, beginning and ending at Fermoyle Strand, is a stiff mix of sandy beach, country lanes, forest tracks, a fine ridge, mountain summits and the magnificent, sweeping valley of Maghanaboe.

Route Description

From the car park at Fermoyle Strand, walk along the sandy beach with Brandon Bay to your left for some 4km. Veer right at a gap through grass-covered sand dunes at **Q 586**₆₆ **134**₄₅. Follow the sandy path to reach a tarmac road. Reach a junction signposted 'Golf Club' on the left. Ignore that and continue straight ahead. Pass a burial ground on the right and continue to reach a concrete bridge.

Take a left at the fork just after the bridge and follow the road to pass a farmhouse. Shortly after crossing the Killiney River, turn right at a junction by a cluster of buildings. Continue along the minor road for around 650m to reach the R560 at a T-junction. Cross the R560 with care to arrive at a metal gate at a forest entrance.

Note: If you are parked in Stradbally or at the roadside viewpoint along the R560, simply walk along the road back towards Tralee for around 1.5–2.2km to reach the metal gate at the forest entrance.

Go through the gate and continue along the broad, surfaced forest track to reach a barrier and another metal gate at a bend. Follow the track as it leads gradually uphill through a mature spruce and pine forest to reach a fork at **Q 601**₅₉ **114**₉₃.

Veer left at the fork and continue along the forest track. On the left are views of the Magharees and Brandon Bay. The tracks then veers south, with the sea now behind you, and rises to a broad lay-by on the left. Hills soon appear ahead as the forest track veers west, the sea now to your right.

Continue along the broad track to reach two transmission masts. The track ends here at a metal gate at **Q 598**01 **108**11. Go through the gate and veer left immediately up a slope of grass and heather. Follow an informal and narrow path that runs to the right of the fence to its corner.

Here, continue southward to reach the top of the ridge, with Stradbally Mountain beckoning westwards. With Brandon Bay behind you, turn right and follow the ridge to reach the summit cairn of Stradbally Mountain at **Q587**35 **091**47, with the dark corrie lake of Loch an Choimín below.

From the summit, descend the rocky terrain to a stony col above Loch an Choimín. Then ascend the grassy, stony slope to the summit cairn of Beenoskee, the 'mountain above the wind', at **Q580**62 **088**80. Views of most of the mountains of Dingle and even of Iveragh may be appreciated from Beenoskee's lofty perch.

A steep slope of stones and some grassy patches leads westward, and then north-westward, from Beenoskee. Soon arrive at a broad gap of stones and peat hags, then descend south-south-west – keeping well left of a stream and its tributaries flowing into Maghanaboe valley. Keep the edge of the plateau to your right and follow it to meet a Red Man signpost at **Q 560**45 **072**07 overlooking the top of the valley.

A track cuts diagonally across the valley's yellow-brown slopes, above a ravine and leading to a notch in its north-east corner at **Q 562**50 **076**41. Here, several streams cut deeply into a rock fault tumble down the slopes. This is an idyllic spot.

The rocky and stony col below Stradbally Mountain, heading towards Beenoskee.

The track now leads westwards down into Maghanaboe valley. Walk down the northern end of the ravine, as the stream cuts sharply down the pear-yellow hillside.

As the track veers right, leading north-westwards out of the valley, you will soon arrive above some ruined stone cottages surrounded by stone walls at **Q 556**$_{34}$ **075**$_{30}$. From here, it is a straightforward walk along the track of the valley floor beside the twisting Glennahoo River and under mountainous scree-swept slopes for some 2.5km to reach a junction at **Q 546**$_{11}$ **100**$_{84}$.

Ignore this junction and carry on past a large farmhouse on the right. Ignore a narrow grassy path on the right and continue on the track, now bordered by stone walls overgrown with fern, gorse and moss.

Reach the R560 by a converted farmhouse with dormer windows. Turn left onto the R560 and continue for around 300m to reach a bend. Take care as the R560 is a busy road with no verges. Cross the bridge over the Glennahoo River and continue for around 500m to reach a cross junction.

Take a left here into An Baile Dubh graveyard if you have a car parked there. If not, veer right into a minor road and continue for around 1km to reach a T-junction. Veer right there and continue for another 1.5km to reach the lane leading into Fermoyle Strand. Turn left into the lane back to the start point.

Loch an Choimín below the precipitous northern slopes of Beenoskee, with Brandon Bay beyond.

ROUTE 21:
Bull's Head Loop from Kinard

Explore one of the finest coastal stretches of cliffs, coves and sea stack along the Wild Atlantic Way in south Dingle.

Grade:	3
Distance:	7km (4¼ miles)
Ascent:	400m (1,312ft)
Time:	3–4 hours, time added for the rough ground between Sea Hill and Doonties Commons.
Map:	OSi 1:50,000 Sheet 70

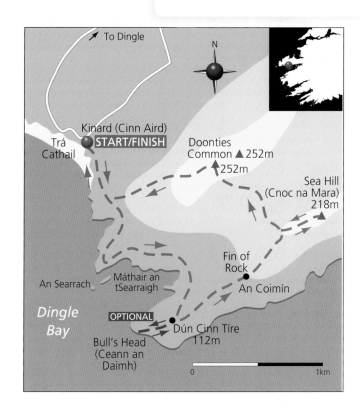

Start/finish: From Dingle town, travel on the N86 for a little over 6.5km (4 miles) towards Lispole, then leave it and veer right onto the L8055 to Kinard (Cinn Aird). If driving from Lispole, veer left around 2.5km (1½ miles) after passing through the village. At the junction into the L8055 there is a signpost for the Irish republican revolutionary Tomás Aghás (1885–1917), who was born in Kinard. Cross a narrow bridge over the Owenalondrig River; then take a sharp left shortly after. On reaching a junction, veer right and then almost immediately left, following signs for Seacrest Hostel. The road is now very narrow and soon veers right to descend toward Trá Chathail strand at Kinard. There are spaces at a small lay-by above the beach at **V 489**$_{11}$ **988**$_{59}$, with Dingle Bay below to the left.

Lispole (Lios Póil) is a small village dating from the nineteenth century. Known as the 'Gateway to the Gaeltacht', it consists mainly of the two parishes of Kinard (Cinn Aird) and Minard (An Mhin Aird). Lispole is encircled to the north by mountainous ground and to the south by the sea cliffs and coves of Dingle Bay. North of the N86 is the Lispole Viaduct, an impressive feat of engineering on the Tralee-to-Dingle Railway, 51.5km (32 miles) long, which was opened in 1891. This narrow-gauge railway was never in profit. It closed around 1939 to passengers and eight years later to general freight. This route explores the quiet coastal area of Bull's Head (Ceann an Daimh), an impressive stretch of the Wild Atlantic Way. Its coast is guarded by precipitous sea cliffs and adorned with beautiful coves. The remote sea stack of An Searrach ('The Foal') can be admired from the top of one of the headlands. The two hillocks of Sea Hill/Cnoc na Mara (218m/715ft) and Doonties Common (Na Dúnta Thiar) (252m/827ft) are also visited, both good vantage points from which to appreciate the beauty of the surrounding area.

Route Description

From the lay-by, head back the way you came for a few metres, then ahead onto a tarmac lane leading down to the beach. The beach is a popular spot for sea anglers and photographers. After just a few metres, step up the steep grassy embankment on the left just before a ring buoy. Continue with care along the narrow grassy strip on the top of the embankment, aiming for an obvious gap in the fence ahead.

Enter a grassy field through the gap and, keeping a fence and the sea to your right, follow a low stone wall gradually uphill. Cross a small stream, then persevere through a short boggy section before rising to meet the corner of a stone wall at **V 491**$_{37}$ **985**$_{12}$.

Cross the stone wall at its corner and follow it, keeping Dingle Bay to your right. There are fine views back the way you came, across Trá Chathail

Skirting around the broad cove and heading towards Bull's Head, with Doonties Commons (left) ahead and Sea Hill (right) in the distance.

strand and the cove of Rinn na bhFaoileann toward Doonsheane and Ballymacadoyle Hill.

As height is gained, skirt around a small cove guarded by steep sea cliffs before veering south-south-west down a grassy slope along a pointed headland which narrows at its tip. The sea stack of An Searrach rises from Dingle Bay below, and can be admired from a rocky perch on the tip of the headland. The drops are precipitous here, so take extra care.

The cove to the east is broader compared to the one on the west of the headland. The plump finger of Bull's Head (Ceann an Daimh), our next objective, can be seen across this cove and the rocky hump of Máthair an tSearraigh.

Leaving An Searrach behind, ascend north-eastward at first, then skirt around the broad cove, keeping the sea to your right at all times. The ground is rough and boggy in places and soon you will see a waterfall that plunges down to the bottom of the cove towards its eastern end.

Cross the stream that runs down the waterfall around 100–150m away from its edge. Pick your spot and take care as you prepare to cross as the terrain is uneven and littered with holes. The ground is rough after crossing the stream. Ascend and then follow a stone wall higher up, where the underfoot terrain improves. The stone wall is the remnant of an ancient promontory fort, and runs along the cliff edge. Take care especially on a windy day and stay away from the cliff edge, as the drops are very steep.

Ancient wedge tombs can be found on the slope before the final pull up to point 112m at Bull's Head.

The view along this stretch is magnificent, particularly to the north-west across the cove toward An Searrach, and south-west down the grassy and rocky slope to the craggy tip and sea arch of Bull's Head.

From point 112m, head north-east to Sea Hill along a broad ridge. There are sheep paths and a rather large fin of rock at **V 502**36 **978**45 if you need reassurance in the mist. Follow a vague, informal path through the gorse and bracken, then a line of rocks to reach a spur. On the top of the spur, veer right for around 200m to reach the summit of Sea Hill.

Descend the summit the way you came. Bypass a rough patch of thick gorse to its right near the end of the spur, and then descend north-west into the grassy col between Sea Hill and Doonties Commons. The ground is very rough here. Cross a fence at the col near a stream, not far away from a sheep's pen away to your left.

Cross another fence and then ascend a rough slope to reach a jumble of rocks at point 252m. Note that twin summit and trig point of Doonties Common is around 250m away from here to the north-east if you wish to visit it.

If not, descend south-westwards down the spur, aiming to reach the corner of the stone wall crossed earlier at **V 491**37 **985**12. Retrace your steps from here and descend back to the start.

Looking across the cove at Bull's Head towards the sea stack of An Searrach and the impressive Kinard coastline.

ROUTE 22:

Knockbrack– Beenduff Ridge

Enjoy superb views over
Castlemaine Harbour and
beyond on a seldom visited
ridge in the Slieve Mish
Mountains.

Grade:	3
Distance:	11.5km (7¼ miles)
Ascent:	510m (1,673ft)
Time:	3¾–4¾ hours
Map:	OSi 1:50,000 Sheet 71

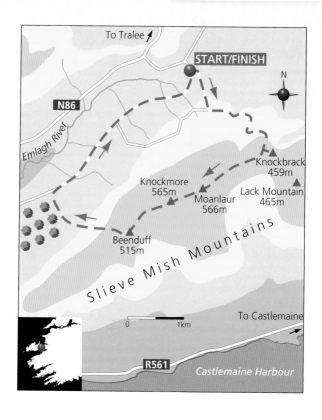

Start/finish: Leave the N86 around 5km (3 miles) from the village of Camp by turning left onto a minor road at **Q 679**₀₀ **067**₅₀. Continue for around 800m (½ mile) until reaching a fork. Take the right fork, drive through a metal gate and along a narrow lane to reach a junction around 200m further at **Q 687**₆₂ **064**₆₃. Park there by a track which veers left at the junction.

The view toward Caherconree from the slopes of Moanlaur.

This route explores a broad, low-lying ridge on the western end of the Slieve Mish Mountains. It is separated from the main Slieve Mish range by a broad saddle between Lack Mountain and Caherbla. Four summits are visited along the ridge: Knockbrack (459m/1,506ft), Moanlaur (566m/1,857ft), Knockmore (565m/1,854ft) and Beenduff (515m/1,690ft). The ridge runs above the length of Castlemaine Harbour to the south, a popular spot for birdwatching or trout fishing. In Irish, *Caisleán na Mainge* means 'castle on the River Maine' and is famed in song as the legendary birthplace of Jack Duggan, the 'Wild Colonial Boy', in 1806.

Route Description

Walk eastward along the track and arrive at a T-junction after about 200m. Take a right here and continue for another 700m along the straight track. A fence and conifers are on the left and a vast expanse of moorland to the right. The track gradually rises to reach a crossroad at **Q 691**₀₄ **058**₀₄.

Take a left at the crossroad and go through a metal gate. Follow the track beyond, keeping the conifers to the left. Shortly after the end of the conifers, reach a junction on the right at **Q 693**₇₂ **057**₈₀ along a boggy section of the track. Turn right here and follow the eroded track. It bends left to reach a metal gate and then crosses a stream. Beyond the stream, the broad, bulldozed track is firmer and stony underfoot as it rises up the

Looking west toward the valleys and mountains of the Dingle Peninsula, with the Emlagh ridge to the left, from the slopes of Beenduff.

hillside. Just after a sharp left bend, reach a grassy lay-by on the right at **Q 698**₂₄ **054**₂₆.

Ascend an indistinct path at the nearer end of the lay-by. The ground rises quite steeply to meet another path just above. Turn left along this grassy, mossy path and follow it, persevering through overgrown sections.

The path gradually meets the top of a spur around 500m further. Turn right on the spur and ascend southward up the grassy slope. An indistinct path leads to the top of a broad grassy ridge. Veer left on the ridge to reach the summit of Knockbrack (*An Cnoc Breac*, 'the speckled hill'), whose flat top is marked by outcrops of rock adorned with heather.

The top of Knockbrack is an ideal place to appreciate the Slieve Mish Mountains to the east, whose slopes spread like an eagle's wings from Gearhane to Caherbla (point 586m on the OSi map) over Caherconree. There are some old mine workings in a hollow below Knockbrack at Coumastabla.

The next 3km or so traverse the broad, boggy and trackless ridge from Knockbrack to Beenduff (point 515m on the OSi map), via the tops of Moanlaur (*Móin Láir*, 'middle bog') and Knockmore (*An Cnoc Mór*, 'the great hill'). Simply continue south-westward along the undulating ridge until reaching the cairn on the heathery summit of Beenduff (An Bhinn Dubh, 'the black peak') at **Q676**₉₇ **036**₅₈.

The view along the entire section of this ridge and particularly at Beenduff is immensely satisfying. Admire the coastline around Castlemaine Harbour to the south, with the pointed fingers of Inch and Cromane. The distant foothills and mountains of the Iveragh Peninsula sweep the background to the south in a glorious panorama. To the west of Dingle, fold upon fold of hills form the backdrop of an expansive valley.

The view across Castlemaine Harbour toward the Iveragh Peninsula from the summit of Beenduff.

Here above the waters of Castlemaine Harbour, let us continue with the tale of the Wild Colonial Boy. In 1824, aged 18, Jack Duggan was convicted of the 'intent to commit a felony' and sentenced to transportation to New South Wales in Australia. In between working on a chain gang, Duggan was assigned to work on farms on two occasions and managed to escape on both. In 1827, along with two other convicts, named Kilroy and Smith, Duggan was caught stealing bullock drays and sentenced to be hanged. Kilroy and Smith were executed but Duggan managed to flee. Over the next few years, he set up a gang of escaped convicts, robbing the rich in Robin Hood style. The gang were known as 'The Strippers' because they stripped the people they robbed of everything they possessed – including their clothes! A special unit was formed to hunt Duggan's gang. Finally, on 1 September 1830, they were caught by Trooper Muggleston's men and Duggan was shot in the head in crossfire.

Leaving the 'Wild Colonial Boy' and the ridge behind, descend west/north-west on a moderately steep slope from Beenduff. As height is lost, a patch of forestry comes into view to the left in the Glanmore valley below. Aim for the eastern boundary of this forest and pick up an informal path on its lower slopes around **Q 664**₆₅ **041**₀₀. Note this path is around 150m away from the forest boundary.

Follow the intermittent path gradually downhill for around 350m to reach a narrow, potholed boreen (marked as The Dingle Way on the map). Turn right and walk along the boreen for some 3.75km or so back to the junction at the start.

ROUTE 23:
Derrymore Horseshoe

Easily the best circuit in the
Slieve Mish Mountains! So
close to Tralee, yet a world
apart.

Grade:	4
Distance:	11km (6¾ miles)
Ascent:	930m (3,051ft)
Time:	4¼–5¼ hours
Map:	OSi Sheet 71

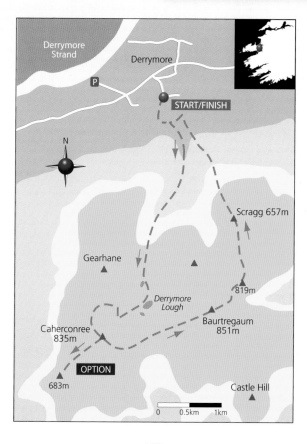

START/FINISH: Take a left turn after Derrymore Bridge at **Q 740**₅₀ **110**₉₀ on the N86 from Tralee. Take the right fork soon after and drive on for another 300m until a right-hand bend in the lane. Park here with consideration along the side of the lane at **Q 742**₃₈ **107**₆₈. Should spaces be limited, then park somewhere along the N86 or at Derrymore Strand.

Looking north toward Derrymore Lough from conglomerate boulders at the head of Derrymore Glen.

Slieve Mish is a mountain range named after Mis, a Milesian princess who was driven to insanity after her father perished during a battle around 1600 BC. Before the Norman invasion, as many as seven bloody battles were said to have been fought around its mountainous flanks. This walk explores the southernmost depths of Derrymore Glen, deep in the heart of these mountains. It is a stunning amphitheatre: remote valleys that rise and rise again, full of boulder-filled dens and each time revealing a lake. We take in a horseshoe of peaks: Caherconree (835m/2,740ft), Baurtregaum (851m/2,792ft) and Scragg (657m/2,156ft) on a route that is world apart from the nearby town of Tralee.

Route Description

From the start point at **Q 742**₃₈ **107**₆₈, walk along the lane, following the bend uphill and pass a yellow-walled house on your right. The tarmac gives way to a green road. The green road bends right and soon there is a metal gate with a stile at **Q 741**₇₂ **106**₉₉. Beyond the stile, a stony track leads uphill and meets The Dingle Way about 300m further. Turn left onto The Dingle Way, follow it for about 200m until it meets a stream with a wooden platform and a yellow marker post at **Q 743**₅₅ **103**₈₄.

The view northeastwards from the summit of Caherconree: the top of Gearhane (left) is visible, and the townland of Fenit beyond the sea inlet.

A valley rears up southward. Pass some ruins; there is also a line of fences further to the left. Follow a grassy, mossy path which heads south-eastward initially, but after about 250m veers southward as you pass under a rocky crag on your right at **Q744**₈₃ **102**₂₇. The path is now scattered with stones and rocks as it leads uphill. A stream flows on the left in a deep ravine. The slope eases somewhat as the towering shapes of Scragg and summit 723m loom ahead.

It is now a gradual ascent as cliffs at the end of the valley come into view. A stream tumbles from the col between summit 723m and Scragg on the left and joins the Derrymore River. Follow the main river upstream, keeping it on your left, and walk deeper into Derrymore Glen.

Cliff columns above on your right project like dragon's scales. You are now walking under the scree-covered slopes of Gearhane. The valley ahead opens up like a lost world. You will soon pass a drystone-wall enclosure at **Q 740**₉₅ **089**₂₃ by some sparkling cascades. The band of cliffs at the end of the glen appears much larger as you walk toward its end.

You eventually arrive near a stream at **Q 739**₄₂ **081**₃₃. Follow a stony path to the right of the stream until it forks. Lovely cascades tumble down to the right of a lake nestled in a rocky niche. Cross the stream on a stony area at the lake and head south-eastward to enter a stunning glacial amphitheatre.

Skirt around the lake's edge, keeping the stream on your left, to reach the ruins of a stone wall at **Q 739**₈₆ **079**₉₄. Walk to the bottom of a jumble of conglomerate boulders ahead. Pick a line southward up its steep slopes to enter a higher valley where there is another larger lake flanked by bands of rock, moody crags and menacing cliffs on its southern corner.

Now veer south-westward and ascend into yet another valley amidst some wild rocky scenery: in places there are conglomerate boulders the size of houses! There is a relatively level area of grass and rock about 500m away at **Q 735**₆₅ **075**₀₂, ideal for a lunch stop. While at lunch, admire your surroundings: a chaos of boulder-filled dens and glacial erratics. Rock bands and crags guard Caherconree's steep slopes to the west and south. Complex and rocky ground rises to the skyline in the south-east. A steep grassy slope rises up north to meet a spur: this is our next objective.

Ascend boldly northward by zigzagging up the slope to reach a shoulder at **Q 735**₁₁ **076**₈₆. Here, veer westward for a final steep ascent to reach the ridge line at **Q 732**₇₄ **077**₃₁. The view now is all consuming: a string of mountains stretched toward the Atlantic with the Brandon range in the distance and the hills around Anascaul closer at hand.

Follow the broad ridge south on peaty and stony slopes and as it later swings south-eastward. The summit of Caherconree is marked with a cairn and a small standing stone at **Q733**₁₀ **072**₆₀. Its Irish equivalent is Cathair Conraoi or 'stone fort of Cú Roí'. Views down into Derrymore Glen, flanked by Gearhane and Baurtregaum on either end, are good.

There is a promontory fort on its south-western flank, near point 683m at **Q 726**₂₅ **066**₀₁. These stone ruins are said to be the abode of Cú Roí mac Dáire, a figure of the Ulster Cycle. Cú Roí kidnapped a woman called Bláthnaid and kept her imprisoned there. Using magic, he commanded the stone walls to spin, keeping intruders out. But one day Bláthnaid tricked him: she signalled her lover, Cú Chulainn, that the fort's defences were down by pouring milk into the Finglas River which speckled it white. Cú Chulainn and his men burst into the fort and slaughtered Cú Roí. If you wish to descend to these ruins, which is just under 1km from Caherconree's summit, you will lose 150m of height. This diversion will add on about ¾ to 1 hour to the overall walking time.

Otherwise, keep to the cliff edge of Caherconree which descends to a narrow, grassy ridge at **Q 737**₇₈ **071**₄₂. The ridge leads north-eastward towards a broad, stony col. Moderate slopes rise to a broad summit area which is stony and rocky. A trig point surrounded by a ring cairn at **Q749**₈₆ **076**₆₇ marks the summit of Baurtregaum (Barr Trí gCom, or the 'top of the three hollows'). There are several more cairns around the summit area. Two unnamed hollows lie to its south; however, there are three to the north of Baurtregaum, lending meaning to the name. These are Derrymore, which you explored earlier, Derryquay and Curraheen to the north-east.

From the summit, head north-eastward for about 300m until you arrive at a cliff edge. Here, you can peer down into the long, wide hollow of Curraheen, with some tiny lakes trapped on its barren floor. Follow the cliff edge north-eastward down a slight dip and rise to the stone cairn at summit 819m, a subsidiary top of Baurtregaum, at **Q 755**₂₅ **081**₉₂. Descend northward from summit 819m; about 100m away you will arrive at a band of rocks. Veer left here and carefully pick a way down the rock steps and later descend grassy, stony slopes which eventually level off to the grassy and mossy summit of Scragg.

From Scragg, descend north-westward down a steep, rugged spur. The ground is a mix of heather and rocky outcrops, but later it is mainly heather and bracken. There is a faint, intermittent path in places, but this can prove difficult to find in the summer months when the bracken and heather are high.

Just over 1.5km away from the summit of Scragg, having descended the steep, uneven ground, you arrive at a broad grassy path at **Q 745**₆₃ **102**₉₀. About 200m after, the path turns left by a Yellow Man marker near a gorse bush. Descend the path and cross a metal bridge over the Derrymore River. Turn left after the bridge, and walk by a fence with the river now on your left. The path leads to a gate with a latch at **Q 744**₃₃ **103**₈₁. From here, simply walk along The Dingle Way and then retrace your steps back to the start point.

A glimpse of the Curraheen Valley from the eastern slopes of Baurtregaum.

Curraheen Horseshoe

A circuit above the longest valley in the Slieve Mish Mountains to its highest summit.

Grade:	4
Distance:	14.5km (9 miles)
Ascent:	880m (2,887ft)
Time:	5½–6½ hours
Map:	OSi 1:50,000 Sheet 71

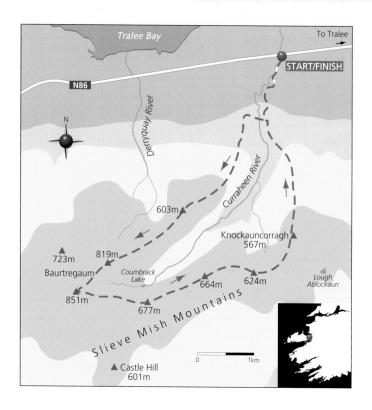

Start/finish: Coming from Tralee, the N86 takes a sharp right bend after Blennerville. Around 2km (1¼ miles) after this bend, leave the N86 and turn left along a lane to park at St Brendan's Church at **Q 786**₉₁ **116**₆₂.

Looking into the Curraheen valley with the cliffs of Gormagh and Glanbrack Mountain at its far end.

The Milesians were believed to be the descendants of Scythian and Egyptian tribes who had fled to the Iberian Peninsula and settled in Spain. According to Irish mythology, they arrived on these shores between 1500 to1700 BC and fought battles with the ruling tribe at that time, the Tuatha Dé Danann. Several kings and queens of the Milesian and Tuatha Dé Danann tribes were killed in the battles. In the end, the Milesians claimed victory and drove the Tuatha Dé Danann underground into forts and mounds. The Slieve Mish range is named after Mis, an ancient Milesian princess around 1600 BC. This route traces a high-level circuit above the longest valley in the Slieve Mish Mountains: Curraheen. Measuring over 4km (2½ miles) from its head to The Dingle Way, the Curraheen valley is characterised by a river twisting across its length. Its source is the tiny Coumbrack Lake, nestled under some cliffs east of Baurtregaum (851m/2,792ft) – the highest mountain in this range, and the high point of our route.

Looking down on the Curraheen valley and Coumbrack Lake from eastern slopes below Baurtregaum.

Route Description

Keep the church on the right and walk to a small car park at its rear, also on the right. Continue along a boreen until reaching a zinc-roofed cottage at the end. Go through the turnstile by a metal gate ahead and follow a track uphill.

The track passes a concrete building and a reservoir on the right, and soon dwindles to a path. Follow the path gradually uphill on short grass and scattered rock. Meet a signpost further uphill at **Q 783**34 **105**98 by a pool of water. (Note this spot as you return to it later.) Turn right there along a track, following a sign for 'Dingle'.

This track is actually part of The Dingle Way, a 162km/101-mile walking trail around the Dingle Peninsula. Soon after, cross a footbridge with metal handrails over the Curraheen River. Around 250m afterwards, the track intersects the base of a grassy spur which rises to the left. Turn left here at **Q 780**42 **106**84 by a large slab of rock, and ascend the spur along an intermittent path.

Reach a grassy shoulder after around 300m by the remnants of an old stone wall. Continue to ascend the slope ahead, which is grassy at first before turning heathery. The heather can be deep in places and if it gets too awkward, veer slightly right. There are also patches of tall bracken along the slope, which are best avoided.

As height is gained, the heather gets shorter and the slope starts to ease. Depending how far right you have detoured, you will need to veer left and regain the top of the spur. Meet a sheep path at **Q 777**22 **096**40 higher up the slope where all difficulties end.

The view southward across the Curraheen valley, with Castlemaine Harbour and the mountains of the Iveragh Peninsula in the distance.

Continue to reach the cairn at Baurtregaum's Far Northeast Top (summit 603m on the map) where there are good views of Banna Strand, Fenit and Tralee Bay below. Descend to a broad saddle and ascend the grassy slope ahead, passing a rocky outcrop and a small cairn along the way to reach a cairn at point 819m. During this stretch, the Curraheen valley comes into view to the left below, and you will appreciate its length and size from above.

From point 819m, descend south-west to a grassy col then ascend a stony and rocky slope to reach a trig pillar on the summit of Bautregaum (Barr Trí gCom, 'top of the three hollows'). The summit area is flat and rocky, graced by clusters of pink sea thrift in season, and there are some ruins nearby.

Descend eastward from the summit down a stony and grassy ridge, keeping steep ground on the left. The Curraheen valley reappears on the left along this stretch. The ridge doglegs at Point 677m and veers left (north-east) to reach a cairn at **Q 765**21 **075**93.

A stony and rocky stretch gives way to peat hags and moorland as the terrain undulates over points 664m and 624m. Between these points, take care not to go down steep ground at Gormagh North, but instead veer right (east/south-eastward) to point 624m on a rather benign slope. In the mist, there is a cairn at **Q 781**49 **079**42 for reassurance.

Descend to a broad saddle below point 624m, then veer left (northward) soon after to Knockauncorragh, keeping steep ground to your left. The ground is spongy with short grass and moss, coloured with spotted orchid, bog cotton and tormentil in season.

The slope steepens somewhat further downhill, but should pose no problems as the heather is short. Descend northward then later veer north-westward down a broad grassy spur to meet the comfort of The Dingle Way below.

Turn left along The Dingle Way and follow it until reaching the signpost at **Q 783**34 **105**98. Turn right there, following signs for 'Curraheen Main Road 1.5km' and retrace steps back to the start.